Highlights

from

Christian History

Michael L. Gowens

Sovereign Grace Publications

Shallotte, North Carolina

HIGHLIGHTS FROM CHRISTIAN HISTORY
Published by Sovereign Grace Publications
Post Office Box 1150
Shallotte, NC 28459
www.sovgrace.net
sovgracepublications@gmail.com

ISBN 978-1-929635-38-2

Scripture quotations are from the King James Version of the Bible.

Printed in the United States of America

Contents

1
The Importance of Studying Church History

To many people, the very concept of history evokes images of row upon row of musty volumes resting in retirement on the shelves of an old library, while microchips and artificial intelligence take center stage in the real world of daily life. Philip Schaff was not one of those people. Schaff, the author of a notable work on the history of Christianity, once remarked, "*History is and must ever continue to be, next to God's word, the richest foundation of wisdom and sweet guide to all successful practical activity.*" Likewise, the 20th century Swiss historian, Herbert Luthy, wisely remarked, "*Consciousness of the past alone can make us understand the present.*"

Of course, this mindset is the polar opposite of the preference for deconstructionism that is so popular today. In this postmodern age, the aim of academic institutions and religious scholars seems almost exclusively devoted to the task of rewriting and deconstructing history, and to view the past as largely irrelevant.

Few disciplines next to the study of God's word itself, however, are as helpful in terms of developing a strong sense of personal and ecclesiastical identity as the study of church history. In his book *A History of the Christian Church*, Lars Qualben writes, "*Church history brings the student in touch with his spiritual ancestry. A patriotic citizen should know the history of his country because such knowledge makes for better citizenship. A corresponding knowledge of church history makes for better and more intelligent church membership.*"[1]

Further, a study of church history will help a person understand current denominational dynamics. Have you ever wondered about the proliferation of denominations within the Christian tradition? Why is professing Christianity so fragmented? What led to the current variety and diversity of doctrine and practice among people who call themselves Christian? Are these differences material or immaterial? An understanding of church history alone will resolve this dilemma.

In this study, I will attempt to trace the history of the church of the Lord Jesus Christ within the context of developments in the larger Christian community during the past two thousand years. I believe that the church of the Lord Jesus Christ has maintained its identity separate and apart from Catholicism, the Protestant Reformation, and the modern proliferation of unaffiliated, independent and nondenominational groups throughout the centuries.

It is true that many seminal events in Christian history occurred within Catholic and Protestant contexts. Nevertheless, Baptists have maintained a quiet, albeit less visible, witness in every generation. Though Athanasius, Augustine, Thomas Aquinas, Martin Luther, John Calvin, and John Wesley receive most of the press when Christian people talk about history, other individuals and groups like the Donatists, Waldenses, and Welsh Baptists stand perpetually in the background, continuing to faithfully serve the Lord, frequently in obscure places and circumstances, below the radar of these more visible and popular groups.

---

1 Lars Qualben, *A History of the Christian Church*, Thomas Nelson Publishers, 1933.

Contemporary historians define these obscure groups as participants in the Free Church movement. In his book *The Free Church Through the Ages*, the Swedish Baptist scholar and church historian Gunnar Weston writes, "*The process of development which transformed the original Christian congregations into a sacramental authoritarian church took place during the latter portion of the second century.*"[2] This change did not take place without protest. James Stitzinger, a contemporary professor of church history, adds concerning these free churches:

> Many church historians have dismissed as heretics those churches that opposed the institutionalized church. Though some of these groups struggled with doctrinal purity, a closer look reveals that the heretical label in most cases was primarily due to their unwillingness to be loyal to the received tradition of the fathers, not to significant doctrinal weakness. A thorough investigation of these independence is difficult because, for the most part, only the works of those who wrote against them have survived. Such groups include the Montanists (*circa* A.D. 156), Novatians (*circa* A.D. 250), the Donatists (*circa* A.D. 311), all of whom left the official church of their day to pursue the pure church.[3]

This study, however, is not primarily concerned to establish a case for the principle of historical succession. My goal is to familiarize the person in the pew with the key developments, the "highlights" if you please, of Christian history. Our target audience, in other words, is the average believer, not the professional historian or scholar.

---

2 James Stitzinger, "Pastoral Ministry in History" in *Rediscovering Pastoral Ministry*, Word Publishers, 1995, pp. 44-45.

3 Ibid.

I believe that an understanding of the three primary periods of Christian history, the Apostolic/Postapostolic period (A.D. 30 to 600), the Medieval period (A.D. 600 to 1500), and the Modern period (A.D. 1500 to 1900) will aid in this pursuit by framing the study in a workable, historical context. A number of key events in each age will provide a context for interpreting many contemporary issues. That will be our format as we embark on this study.

So why is it important to study Christian history? First of all, church history provides a grid or a framework for interpreting orthodoxy. It helps us understand the formation of Christian doctrine and practice. Secondly, a knowledge of church history also aids to strengthen a sense of identity, to explain current circumstances, and to immunize believers against the repetition of past errors. In a day when many professing Christians are largely rootless and dangerously disconnected with the past, even a rudimentary survey of church history, like this current study, may prove to be extremely helpful to remedying that problem. That is our hope as we proceed.

PART 1

The Apostolic Period

A.D. 30 – 100

2
Acts: The First Thirty Years
A.D. 30 - 60

The history of Christianity begins with the only divinely-inspired church history ever written, the *Acts of the Apostles*. The book of *Acts* records the first thirty years of the history of the church. It covers events from the ascension of Christ to Paul's first imprisonment in Rome.

Acts is the story of the remarkable spread of Christianity from a small nucleus of Jewish believers in Jerusalem to a multicultural movement so far-reaching, both in terms of geographic scope and social influence, that the mighty Roman Empire viewed it as a growing threat.

The inspired narrative begins in Jerusalem with 120 disciples. It concludes with the apostle Paul under house arrest in Rome, Italy, preaching and teaching the gospel to everyone with whom he came into contact. It is the story of how the gospel spread within three short decades, from East to West, from the Jews to the Gentiles, from Asia to Europe.

To what may we attribute the remarkable growth of this fledgling movement? Were the leaders of this movement especially impressive and influential? Did they possess significant wealth to finance great advertising campaigns? Did the early Christians have the endorsement and support of powerful figures? The answer to each of these questions is a resounding "no." The disciples of Jesus were actually unlettered men who came from such common and mundane occupations as the fishing trade, tent making, and tax collecting. Compared to the religious leaders of the day, Jesus' disciples were unlearned and ignorant men (cf. Acts 4:13). Yet, without a bank account to finance them, a military to defend them, or aristocratic influence to win them an audience, these early disciples of Jesus Christ so infiltrated the Mediterranean world with the gospel that people reported, "*These that have turned the world upside down have come hither also*" (Acts 17:6).

That such a ragtag group of fishermen and tax collectors would even succeed in getting this fledgling movement off the ground is surprising. That it would survive and even flourish for three decades is nothing short of phenomenal. In fact, it is supernatural. The growth and progress of the early church is due to the fact that this was no mere human movement. Divine empowerment alone explains the longevity and success of Christianity.

The early Christians were "*endued with power from on high*" at 9:00 a.m. Pentecost morning (cf Lk. 24:49). Convinced that they worshiped One who had been resurrected from the dead, they fearlessly and powerfully proclaimed a message that, for all intents and purposes, was unbelievable. And yet, people by the thousands believed it, embraced it, and committed their lives to proclaiming and spreading it, at the risk of personal loss, physical suffering, and even death.

The inspired account of the church in *Acts* is the prototype of the parable of the mustard seed that grew from a very small and insignificant beginning into a tree so great that the fowls of the air came to lodge in its branches (Mt. 13:31-32).

Peter & the Church at Jerusalem (Acts 1-9)

The book of *Acts* may be divided into two sections. Chapters 1-9 form the first section and describe the church under the leadership of the apostle Peter. With Jerusalem as the center or hub of activity. Peter, the former fisherman, was used by God during the first great in-gathering of converts. He cast the gospel net (Mt. 13:47) into a sea of people gathered at Jerusalem and drew many believers into the militant church.

Jews throughout the Mediterranean world had converged on Jerusalem for the festival of Pentecost. Once the Holy Spirit descended on the apostles, Peter began to preach. His sermon recorded in Acts 2 identified Jesus of Nazareth as the anticipated Messiah and affirmed, by means of an exposition of Psalm 16:8, that he had been resurrected from the dead. The hearers that day, moved by a collective sense that a great sin had been committed in the crucifixion of such a righteous man, as well as a sense of perplexity that could not be satisfied by any of the explanations concocted to account for the missing body of Jesus, were convinced and convicted by Peter's sermon. Three thousand people were baptized and added to the church on that happy day.

In the days and weeks following, new converts were made on a daily basis (Acts 2:47). In time, the Jewish religious leaders determined to put a stop to this increasingly popular movement (Acts 4:15ff). They questioned Peter and John, then threatened them, lest they continue preaching in the name of Jesus. Opposition, however, did not dampen the courageous testimony of the apostles. They continued to preach and God attended their word with signs and wonders. "*And daily in the temple and in every house,*" says Acts 5:42, "*they ceased not to teach and preach Jesus Christ.*"

The Jewish rulers intensified their efforts to stymie these renegades. Stephen died as the first Christian martyr (Acts 7) and an effort to halt the spread of the church was spearheaded by a young lawyer from Tarsus named Saul. Persecution had the effect of dispersing the disciples from Jerusalem into surrounding areas like Samaria. But everywhere the disciples went, they continued to preach the word (Acts 8:4).

In Samaria, Philip baptized both men and women (Acts 8:12), preaching the gospel in many villages of the Samaritans on his way back to Jerusalem (Acts 8:25). On this trip, Philip also baptized a very reputable emissary of Candace, queen of the Ethiopians, who had been up to Jerusalem to worship (Acts 8:26-40).

Nevertheless, the Jewish persecution of those who followed Jesus continued. Saul of Tarsus made havoc of the church, binding the saints and casting them into prison. But the Lord had another plan for Saul. While on his way to Damascus to persecute believers, Saul saw a light brighter than the noonday sun (Acts 9). The risen Christ spoke to him and quickened his hard and obstinate heart. Through Ananias, Christ revealed his will that Saul was his chosen vessel to preach the gospel to the Gentiles. And so the chief opponent of the church became the principal proponent of the glorious gospel for the next twenty years.

The Apostolic Character of the Church

During these early years, the most basic characteristic of the church was established. It is in *Acts* that we learn that the church is an apostolic institution. Ephesians 2:20 indicates that the church is founded "*on the apostles and prophets, Jesus Christ himself being the chief cornerstone.*"

Apostles were directly commissioned by Christ as his official representatives; consequently, their word carried his authority (Lk. 22:29-30). The legitimacy of a particular doctrine or practice in the life of the primitive church was determined by tracing its origin to the apostles (Acts 2:42). The apostles had authority to bind or loose in the confidence that heaven would sanction their decisions (Mt. 16:19).

It is important to emphasize the apostolic character of the early church. Everything the church believes and practices finds precedent in the apostles. The apostolic age sets the pace for both orthodoxy and orthopraxy—for both sound doctrine and sound practice. Any idea or activity that does not conform to apostolic criteria, therefore, is to be dismissed as an innovation of human origin.

It is clear that the test of apostolicity was important to the primitive church. During these early days, it was not uncommon for people to claim apostolic authority in an attempt to gain influence. The risen Christ commends the church at Ephesus because they "*tried them that say they are apostles and are not, and found them liars*" (Rev. 2:2).

One might question, "Why were these people claiming to be apostles?" Well, the answer is obvious. They knew that, because apostolicity was so crucial to ecclesiastical integrity, such a claim was essential if they were to gain the people's loyalty and admiration. If they were indeed apostles, then they had the authority to determine church polity and theology. If they were impostors, then they had no authority beyond a mere effort to disseminate and implement the apostolic pattern of gospel church life.

Why is the apostolic character of the church pertinent to a discussion of church history? This issue is crucial because it is basic and fundamental to the way the church functions. Apostolicity determines how the church is organized, how it functions, and how it should be governed.

There are basically five forms of church government in Christianity's long and storied history: 1. Papal; 2. Episcopal; 3. Presbyterian; 4. Congregational; 5. Apostolic. Baptist people have historically practiced a congregational form of church government under apostolic authority. In other words, Baptists do not practice a purely democratic form of congregationalism in which the majority vote prevails, but they believe that the decisions made by the congregation should be consistent with the teachings prescribed by the apostles in the New Testament.

Roman Catholics observe a papal form of government. They believe that the Pope is the lone successor of the apostles, and therefore exercises apostolic authority to speak in the place of Christ. Anglicans and Episcopalians practice a government in which the church is governed by an archbishop, under whose authority bishops govern a particular diocese, or groups of local churches.

Presbyterians observe a church polity in which a group of Elders exerts authority like a "board of directors" or "leadership team" over a single church. And Congregtionalists practice a polity in which the local church members determine by majority vote that church's direction in faith and practice.

Baptists, again, are not strict Congregationalists, but believe that an ordained Elder is to teach the word to the local church, while a group of qualified Deacons are appointed by the congregation to manage the church's administrative affairs, and the congregation is to decide on issues that arise based on the criteria of the apostolic pattern taught in the New Testament.

The apostolic character of the church is relevant to a discussion of church history because it explains why some, through the centuries, have felt compelled by conscience to withdraw from those who attempted to alter the complexion of church structure, function and worship.

The long history of Christianity is marked by two basic schools of thought. The one believed that the church was the ultimate authority, and the other that the apostles, through the holy scriptures, were the ultimate authority. To say it in other words, the one believed that the church was an organization *in flux*, that is, changing with the times, and the other, that it was an organization that was already fully equipped (both in terms of its doctrine and its discipline) by the apostles of the Lord Jesus Christ.

Hence, when Arius arose in the 3rd century A.D. promoting the idea that Jesus was not co-essential to the Father, or when some promoted clericalism (a class distinction between the clergy and the laity), or the doctrine of purgatory, or distinctions between mortal and venial sins, certain Christian people have, for conscience sake, found it necessary to test such claims by apostolic criteria and to adjudge them departures from the biblical pattern.

In order to continue to pursue a pure church (that is, one that conforms in both doctrine and discipline to the church Jesus Christ built via the apostles), therefore, Christian people through the centuries have been compelled by conscience to withdraw from those that perpetrated these aberrations. Denominationalism, i.e. modern fractures within the many groups that claim to be "Christian," is largely the result of this dynamic.

Paul & the Church at Antioch (Acts 10-28)

The conversion of Paul in Acts 9 marks a turning point in the apostolic period of the church. From this point, Paul's apostolic influence, instead of Peter's, assumes prominence, and Antioch Church, instead of Jerusalem, gradually assumes a central role in early church activity.

That Christ intended his church to grow beyond a mere Jewish context is clear from Acts 1:8: "*And ye shall be witnesses unto me both in Jerusalem, and in Judea, and in Samaria, and unto the uttermost parts of the earth*." When I read that verse, I think of a diagram of concentric circles. The center circle represents Jerusalem. The circle outside of that is Judea. The next circle is Samaria, and then finally the uttermost parts of the earth.

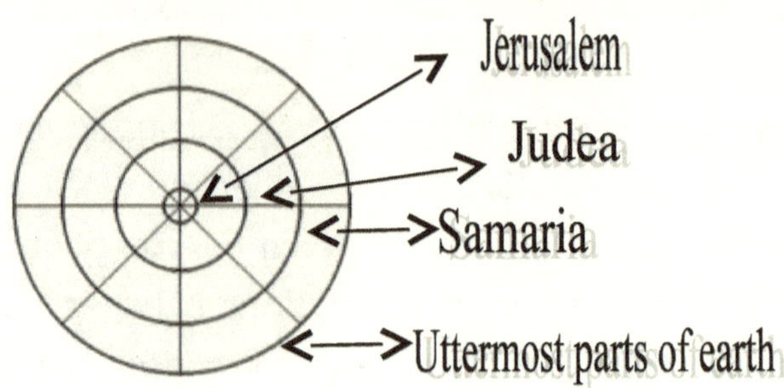

Persecution proved to be the impetus for expanding beyond the city of Jerusalem (Acts 8:1). As persecution intensified, many Christians were dispersed. The early church was decentralized, but like the ancient Hebrews who multiplied the more that Pharaoh attempted to exterminate them, the church only grew as a result of persecution. The dissemination of believers into the outlying regions simply broadened the potential influence of the gospel, and this paved the way for the expansion of the gospel among the Gentiles.

Christ commissioned Paul to be his apostle to the Gentiles (Acts 9:15). Acts 10-28 is almost exclusively devoted to developing the story of the circulation of the gospel among Gentile nations. It is appropriate, therefore, that the final reference to the Apostle Peter's influence within the early church, before his ministry is eclipsed by Paul's, is the story of Gentile centurion's conversion named "Cornelius" (Acts 10).

It is impossible to exaggerate the importance of this cultural shift. Prejudice between the Jews and the Gentiles had risen to a fevered pitch and seemed to be an insurmountable social hurdle. The ethnic tension between the two groups was incredible. To an orthodox Jew, fraternity with a Gentile was taboo. But God knew how to overcome Peter's reluctance and prejudice.

Cornelius was a Gentile whom "God had cleansed" (cf. Acts 10:15), even prior to gospel conversion. He gave evidence by his works of righteousness and pious fear of God, that he had already been born again, even prior to Peter's visit (Acts 10:35). After Peter preached, the household of Cornelius experienced a mini-Pentecost with an effusion of the Holy Spirit comparable to that seminal day (Acts 10:44-46). Cornelius and his family were baptized, and Peter tarried with them certain days following.

When Peter returned to Jerusalem, however, he met with opposition for breaching these cultural barriers (Acts 11:1-3). After he reviewed the details of the story with the brethren, however, they rejoiced that "God also had granted to the Gentiles repentance unto life" (Acts 11:18).

Meanwhile, the dispersed believers traveled to Antioch and preached the Lord Jesus to the Greeks, many of whom believed (Acts 11:19-21). Like a spreading flame, the gospel of Christ could not be contained by social and cultural boundaries. As tidings of these developments reached Jerusalem Church, the apostles dispatched Barnabas to Antioch (Acts 11:22). The evidence of God's grace upon them was conclusive, and Barnabas encouraged them to be loyal and faithful to Christ (Acts 11:23).

Tarsus, the hometown of Paul, was less than 100 miles from Antioch. Though the narrative does not reveal Barnabas' thought process, he left Antioch to seek Saul. When he found him, Barnabas brought him back to Antioch, where they both stayed and ministered for the next year. It was here that the disciples of Jesus were first called "Christians" (Acts 11:26).

It was from Antioch Church that Paul and Barnabas were dispatched to circulate the gospel throughout the Mediterranean world (Acts 13:1-3). They sailed to Cyprus (Acts 13:4), then to Antioch of Pisidia (Acts 13:14). It was there that they entered the Jewish synagogue and Paul began to preach the sermon recorded in Acts 13:16-41. At the conclusion of his sermon, the Gentiles approached him with the request that these words "*might be preached to them the next Sabbath*" (Acts 13:42).

When the next Sabbath day arrived, almost the entire city turned out for preaching. But Paul's sermon was not welcomed by all. The unbelieving Jews contradicted and blasphemed. Paul, however, was undaunted, saying "*It was necessary that the Word of God should first have been spoken to you; but seeing ye put it from you, and judge yourselves unworthy of everlasting life, lo, we turn to the Gentiles*" (Acts 13:46). From this point forward, Paul's evangelistic activity was almost exclusively limited to the Gentiles, and Jewish opposition to the spread of the gospel intensified dramatically.

The First Doctrinal Crisis

It was inevitable that the rapid influx of Gentiles into the early church would cause tension. When some Jewish men visited Antioch Church and insisted that compliance with the Law of Moses was essential to salvation, Paul and Barnabas journeyed to Jerusalem Church to meet with the apostles and elders (Acts 15).

The Council debated the issue. Peter recounted his experience at the house of Cornelius; Paul and Barnabas reviewed their labors among the Gentiles, and James supported Peter's report by quoting from the Old Testament prophet Amos (Acts 15:15-18; Amos 9:11-12), and advised that the apostles hesitate to impose regulations on the Gentile churches, except in the case of a few ethical matters

(Acts 15:20). The subsequent letter detailing certain dietary restrictions and the importance of sexual purity is recorded in Acts 15:20-29.

This official edict from the apostles was the defining moment in the battle to win acceptance for Gentile believers. But some Jews resisted the pressure to immediately abandon their cultural and ethnic biases. Paul labored to be sensitive to these prejudices, and was careful to do nothing that might hinder the progress of the gospel (Acts 16:1-4). When the Judaizers troubled the Galatian churches, however, insisting that Christ's work on the cross must be supplemented by obedience to Moses' law for salvation, Paul identified it as "*another* [that is a different] *gospel*" (Gal. 1:6). His letter to the churches in Galatia is a defense of the message of salvation by grace alone, a message that he terms "*the truth of the gospel*" (Gal. 2:5).

The Macedonian Call

Meanwhile, the westward movement of the church was being orchestrated by the Holy Spirit. When Paul and Timothy planned to go to Asia and Bithynia, "*the Spirit suffered them not*" (Acts 16:6-7). Instead, Paul saw a vision of a man from Macedonia (i.e. northern Greece) imploring his help (Acts 16:9-10). So, they set out at once for Philippi, a chief city of Macedonia.

There they found a woman named Lydia, who believed and was baptized with her family, and whose house became the headquarters of apostolic ministry in that city (Acts 16:11-15). After other converts were baptized and a church was established (the first church on European soil), Paul journeyed to Thessalonica (Acts 17:1-9), Berea (Acts 17:10-15), Athens (Acts 17:16-34), and Corinth

(Acts 18:1-17). He stayed in Corinth for eighteen months, preaching the word and establishing the church in the faith.

A Door Opened in Ephesus

Paul's desire to preach in Asia had been postponed for a couple of years. Now, however, the Holy Spirit was pleased to open a great and effectual door in the important metropolitan city of Ephesus (1 Cor. 16:8-9). He sailed from Corinth with Aquila and Priscilla, leaving them in Ephesus while he returned temporarily to Antioch Church (Acts 18:18-23).

After a brief visit at Antioch, Paul set out for Ephesus via the regions of Galatia and Phrygia, visiting and confirming the churches on the way. Meanwhile, Aquila and Priscilla had located a gifted young preacher named Apollos in Ephesus, to whom they more clearly explained the gospel (Acts 18:24-28). This man would prove to be a great benefit to the churches, especially in Corinth.

When Paul arrived in Ephesus, he first rebaptized a dozen or so men who had only received the baptism of John (Acts 19:1-7). These new Christians became the nucleus of the church in Ephesus.

For two years, Paul utilized the School of Tyrannus, a philosophical debating society, as a platform for advancing the gospel. This popular school proved to be a powerful venue for mass marketing the gospel (Acts 19:10). In Ephesus, the truth triumphed over the superstitions of magic (Acts 19:19) and idolatry (Acts 19:23-41), and a strong church, which would later become the hub of post-apostolic activity, was established. It was an emotional scene when Paul finally departed Ephesus Church to return to Jerusalem, never to see their faces again (Acts 20:17-38).

The Gospel Spreads to Italy

Though many of Paul's friends advised him against returning to Jerusalem, he would not be deterred (Acts 21:4-13). The climate in that city was now extremely hostile toward Christians, but God intended to use his servant Paul to spread the gospel deep into Europe.

Paul was arrested in Jerusalem and brought before a court (Acts 21:27-40). When they began to scourge him, Paul retorted with a question that put them on notice of legal jeopardy, asking if it was lawful for them to beat a Roman citizen, for he had been "freeborn" (Acts 22:25-29). Paul eventually appealed to Caesar and was transported, in an extremely treacherous sea voyage, to Rome, where he was placed under house arrest.

The Book of Acts concludes with Paul preaching to everyone with whom he came into contact for the space of two whole years (Acts 28:30-31). Within these first thirty years of Christian history, the gospel and the church that existed to propagate it had made its way, in the providence of God, from its small origins in Jerusalem all the way across the Mediterranean Sea to Rome, Italy, in western Europe.

3
The Apostolic Church from Paul to John A.D. 60 - 100

For the next forty years, the early church continued to expand its influence throughout Asia Minor (modern Turkey) and eastern and western Europe. But with the spread and increasing visibility of the Christian gospel came an intensification of the pressure of external persecution.

The Beginning of Roman Persecution (A.D. 60-70)

Persecution during the first thirty years of Christian history came primarily from religious Jews. Persecution from secular sources like the Roman emperors was rare, for they considered Christians to be merely another Jewish sect, and the Jewish religion enjoyed legal status in the empire. This changed, however, in A.D. 64.

Nero, the "Augustus" mentioned in Acts 25:21, was losing popularity when, on the night of July 18, A.D. 64, a disastrous fire broke out in Rome and raged for almost an entire week.[1] Ten of the fourteen regions of the city were destroyed. Nero was vacationing in Antium[2] when the fires began, but returned to the capital city as reports arrived that the fire was approaching his personal contruction project. Upon his return, he organized a significant firefighting effort. His tardy response, however, could not stop the rumors that "Nero fiddled while Rome burned," nor the spread of popular

1 Tacitus, *Annals*, 15:39.

2 Antium, modern-day Anzio, was Nero's birthplace. It is situated about 35 miles south of Rome and a favorite seaside villa where wealthy Romans escaped the intense summer heat.

conspiracy theories implicating the emperor for deliberately setting the fires to boost his own political popularity.

It soon became evident to Nero that to deflect public suspicion that he was responsible for the arson, he would have to implicate someone else. So Nero blamed the fire on the Christians. Christians had recently evoked public suspicion because of their refusal to worship the emperor, their separate way of life, and their secret meetings. They were an easy target and Nero immediately launched a campaign of persecution against them affecting a radical change in the news-cycle.

Some Christians were dressed in furs and killed by dogs, and others were dipped in pitch and used as human torches to illumine his gardens near the *Mons Vaticanus* ("Vatican Hill"). Nero also seized the occasion to slay the two most visible leaders of the early church. According to early Christian tradition, together with reports of post-apostolic "fathers" such as Clement of Rome (*circa* 96 A.D.), Ignatius of Antioch, Irenaeus and Tertullian (late 1st to early 3rd centuries), the Apostle Peter was martyred by crucifixion at this time, and the Apostle Paul was beheaded in *circa* 64 A.D. on the Ostian Way, just outside the city of Rome.

The Roman historian Tacitus described the grisly circumstances as follows:

> Nero punished with the utmost refinement of cruelty a class hated for their abominations who are commonly called Christians. *Christus*, from whom their name is derived, was executed at the hands of Pontius Pilate in the reign of Tiberius in Rome. An immense multitude was convicted, not so much on the charge of arson as because of their hatred of the human race. Besides being put to death, they were made to serve as objects of amusement.

> They were clad in the hides of beasts and torn to pieces by dogs. Others were crucified. Others set on fire to illumine the night when the daylight faded.

Tacitus proceeded to acknowledge that the Christians were destroyed not for the public good, but to gratify the cruelty of an individual. Why were Christians such easy targets for Roman persecution? Why were they, as Tacitus said, "hated for their abominations"? Three primary reasons for the growing secular disdain of Christianity might be cited.

1. They refused to acknowledge the Roman pantheon. Christians were monotheists in a polytheistic society. They believed in only one God revealed in Jesus Christ (Deut. 6:4; 1 Tim. 2:5). Conscience would not permit them, therefore, to engage in the rituals that were such an important part of Roman society, such as burning a pinch of incense before the bust of Caesar and confessing *Kaiser Kyrios* ("Caesar is Lord"), or sacrificing to some deity for the welfare of the state. Their lack of tolerance and refusal to acknowledge the gods appeared arrogant and unpatriotic to the Romans, who called them "atheists."

2. Their rites and ceremonies were misunderstood. They called one another "brother" and "sister" and claimed to love one another. The Romans mistook this for an endorsement of incest. Further, they shared the Lord's Supper in a closed setting. As rumors spread that they ate the flesh and drank the blood of Christ, they were accused of cannibalism. The growing sense that Christianity was a dangerous cult could not be quelled.

3. They challenged the social order. The Christian concern to treat male and female, slave and freeman, Jew and Greek as equals was viewed by the Romans as subversive. It undermined the class structure on which Roman society was built.

Nero was the first secular leader to distinguish Christians as a separate class from the Jews. But in the general opinion of the public, there was little difference between the church and the synagogue up to this point. That perspective would radically change, once and for all, in A.D. 70.

While Nero was persecuting Christians in Rome, Florus, a new Roman procurator arrived in Judea in A.D. 64. This heavy-handed ruler made it his mission to beat the Jews into shape. Judea had been a troublesome province for too long. In one day in A.D. 66, Florus' soldiers slaughtered 3,600 Jews in Jerusalem.

The result was the First Jewish Revolt.[3] Jewish rebels attacked Roman strongholds in Jerusalem and Galilee. Hearing of the revolt, Nero sent his leading general, a man named Vespasian, and 60,000 soldiers to retake Galilee and Jerusalem. As Vespasian prepared to attack, however, he received news of Nero's death. Vespasian returned to Rome and was crowned emperor in Nero's place.

He didn't forget his mission, however, for in the spring of A.D. 70, Vespasian sent an army, under the leadership of a general named Titus, to besiege Jerusalem. Between August 5th and 8th of that year,

3 The Jewish historian Flavius Josephus blames Florus for sparking this open revolt against Roman rule.

Jerusalem fell. One million Jews were killed and 98,000 were led into captivity. The temple was leveled to the ground. Only one wall in the Temple Mount, the "Wailing Wall," remained.

After the fall of Jerusalem, Jewish synagogues throughout the Mediterranean world refused to admit Christians to their services any more, and synagogue prayers regularly incorporated a curse against "the Nazarenes." The break between the church and her Jewish religious ancestry was complete.

The Apostle John and Ephesus Church (A.D. 70-100)

In the latter part of the first century, the Apostle John emerged from obscurity to exert a wide and deep influence over the churches. Elders C. B. and Sylvester Hassell write, "According to the testimony of Clement of Alexandria and Irenaeus, Saint John, after the death of Saint Peter and Saint Paul, took up his residence at Ephesus. No city could have been better chosen as a center from which to watch over the churches and follow closely the progress of heresy. It was there that false Gnosticism,[4] first of all, showed itself and perpetually sought new Adherents. The Apostle Paul had spoken before his death of its rapid progress (1 Tim. 6:20-21). In his second epistle to Timothy (2 Tim. 1:15-18), he seems to point out Ephesus as the city most threatened with heresy, where consequently the presence of an apostle would be especially needed...Ephesus was the center of his apostolic activity, but that activity extended over a wide area."[5]

---

4 An idea combining Platonic philosophy, Alexandrian Judaism, and various mystic religions with Christianity.

5 *History of the Church of God*, C. B. & Sylvester Hassell, pp. 241-242.

Domitian (A.D. 81-96) was the Roman emperor while John ministered to the churches. Domitian demanded the title "Lord and God" and made emperor worship the official religion of the Roman

Empire. John was among the exiles that Domitian sent to Patmos[6] in approximately A.D. 96, probably because of his refusal to acknowledge Domitian's self-proclaimed divine status.

It was there that John wrote the *Book of Revelation.* Elder Hassell says of this book: "It was written during a time of persecution...Contrasting the glory of the church above with the indignities heaped on the church below, the Revelation seems to drown the cries and the blasphemies of earth in the songs of the blessed and of the angels. After depicting the conflict and the sufferings of the saints and the terrible judgments of God upon their persecutors, it opens a vista of the heavenly places. It is one of the grandest conceptions of the sacred writer, perpetually linking together earth and heaven, and showing in the events of religious history the counterpart of other events, of which the abode of the blessed is the scene."[7]

The *Book of Revelation* concerns both things "*which must shortly come to pass*" (Rev. 1:1) and "*things which must be hereafter*" (Rev. 4:1). That is to say, the book has both an immediate, historical application to Christian people who were John's contemporaries, and a more long-range, prophetic application to believers who would live in subsequent ages. In terms of its immediate value, the struggle

6 A small rocky island off the coast of Asia Minor in the Aegean Sea.

7 Hassell, pp. 247-248.

between Christianity and the Antichrist, depicted in the context of the church's ultimate triumph through Christ, would prove very salutary to the Christians in Asia Minor near the end of the 1st century, as well as to Christians who would live in the 2nd century, for 90-200 A.D. would prove to be both an age of intense persecution and an age of insidious doctrinal corruption. Elder Hassell writes again, "The church has not only to fight against Antichrist without; it has also to resist Antichrist within; to do battle, that is, with heresy and false prophecy."[8]

This two pronged attack upon the church from the devil, i.e. external persecution from the secular world, and internal tension from the influence of false doctrine, would characterize the next few centuries in the history of the church.

Following Domitian, the Roman emperors Trajan and Marcus Aurelius would carry out massive campaigns of persecution against Christians, forcing many Christian people to flee to the catacombs, an elaborate system of tunnels beneath the city of Rome, for asylum. If outward pressure were not enough, the church would encounter a serious challenge from within in the form of the *Gnostic* heresy. The post-apostolic age of the church would be no walk in the park. These would truly be "the times that try men's souls."

8 Hassell, p. 249.

PART 2

The Post-Apostolic Period

A.D. 100 – 600

4
Persecution in the Post-Apostolic Era A.D. 100 - 200

Much of the information that survives concerning the 2nd century in church history concerns the sufferings of Christians. This leads us to believe that the primary characteristic of this period was persecution.

After Domitian, Trajan assumed power as the new Roman Emperor. He appointed Pliny the Younger as governor of Bithynia and charged him to investigate the worrisome new sect who were called Christians. The letters between Pliny and Trajan provide a snapshot not only of the character of early Christian people, but also the kind of pressure they were forced to endure. The year was approximately 112 A.D.

Pliny first details the practice of the early Christians:

> On an appointed day, the Christians are accustomed to meet at daybreak and to recite or sing a hymn to Christ as to a god and to bind themselves by a sacramentum or oath to abstain from theft and robbery, adultery, and breach of faith. After this, they depart and meet again to take food. To find out the truth concerning them, I applied torture to two maidservants who were called deaconesses, but I found nothing but a depraved and extravagant superstition.

Next, Pliny revealed his method of dealing with them.

> This is the course that I have adopted. I ask them if they are Christians. If they admit it, I repeat the question a second and a third time, threatening capital punishment. If they persist, I sentence them to death, for their inflexible obstinacy should certainly be punished. Christians who are Roman citizens are reserved to be sent to Rome. I discharged those who were willing to curse Christ, a thing which, it is said, genuine Christians cannot be persuaded to do.

In his reply, Trajan endorsed Pliny's strategy of dealing with them, but advised him not to seek them out for punishment. Only if someone complained against them should Pliny pursue them for justice. Seizing on an opportunity to make money, "informants" flooded Asia Minor and turned the business of gathering intelligence on the Christians into a lucrative trade.

Now previous to A.D. 100, the persecution that Christians had endured was principally intramural, from the Judaizers. But now, the persecution arose from the secular society. We learn from the *Book of Revelation,* written by the apostle John near the end of the first century, that secular persecution against the Christians was already beginning as the first century was drawing to a close. Revelation 2:9 speaks of the church at Smyrna who was already enduring "*blasphemy,*" the Lord says, "*from them which say they are Jews and are not, but are of the synagogue of Satan.*" After acknowledging the pressure they were currently experiencing, the Lord warns this church, "*Fear none of those things which thou shalt suffer. Behold, the devil shall cast some of you into prison, that you may be tried, and you shall have tribulation ten days. Be thou faithful unto death, and I will give thee a crown of life*" (v. 10). So he anticipates that more persecution was coming.

Likewise, in Revelation 2, it speaks of the church at Pergamos where a member of that church named Antipas is called “my faithful martyr” (Rev. 2:13). Some had already died at the hands of secular authorities because of their Christian faith.

Ignatius of Antioch was martyred early in the second century. Trajan himself interviewed Ignatius in approximately 115 A.D. The conversation between them went as follows:

> Trajan: There you are wicked devil, deceiver of men.
> Ignatius: Not an evil spirit, but I have Jesus Christ in my heart.
> Trajan: Jesus Christ within you? Do you mean him who was crucified by Pontius Pilate?
> Ignatius. Yes. He was crucified for my sins.

The Colosseum in Rome, a 3-tiered amphitheatre capable of seating 45,000 spectators

At this, Trajan sentenced Ignatius to be taken to Rome and thrown to the wild beasts in the Colosseum, a three tiered amphitheater capable of seating 45,000 spectators. Ignatius responded to the sentence by saying, “I thank thee, O Lord, that thou hast vouchsafed this to honor me.” In the Colosseum, Ignatius said, “I am God's grain to be ground between the teeth of wild beasts so that I may be a holy loaf for the Lord.”

Like Ignatius, in A.D. 155, Polycarp, pastor of the church at Smyrna, was apprehended by the authorities. After feeding those who came to take him into custody, Polycarp surrendered himself with the words, "God's will be done." At the judgment seat, the governor begged Polycarp to consider himself: "Have respect for your old age. Say, 'Away with the atheists'." Polycarp beckoned to the crowd of spectators and said, "Away with the atheists." The governor said, "I have wild beasts. If you refuse, I will throw you to them." Polycarp replied, "Send for them." The consul said, "If you despise the wild beasts, I will send you to the fire. Swear, and I will release you. Curse Christ." Polycarp responded, "Eighty and six years have I served Christ, and he has done me no wrong. How then can I blaspheme my King who saved me?"

When the torch was applied to the wood, Polycarp prayed aloud, "Lord God, Father of our blessed Savior, I thank thee that I have been deemed worthy to receive the crown of martyrdom and that I may die for thee and for thy cause."

Polycarp, again, pastored the church in Smyrna and was the last living connection to the apostle John. A man named Irenaeus, who grew up in a Christian family in Smyrna, was privy to the preaching and teaching of Polycarp. Irenaeus later became pastor in Lyon in Southern France. He is best remembered as the earliest advocate of the idea that each of the four *Gospels,* as recorded in the New Testament canon, were essential, together with his doctrinal stance against the *Gnostics* and followers of Valentinus. His well known book entitled *Against Heresies* was a defense against *Gnostic* teaching. In that book, Irenaeus traces *Gnosticism* back to the magician Simon Magus, who is referenced in Acts 8, and he insists that the *Gnostic* teaching that the material world is evil and only spirit is good is the essence of paganism, not Christianity. Little is known about Irenaeus' death. Some believe he died as a martyr in A.D. 202.

It was during this time of great persecution that Christians saw the need to explain themselves in light of the charges that were being brought against them. A number of scholars assumed the role of apologist[1] for the Christian faith. These men did not primarily aim to convert outsiders, but to give a defense of the practices and beliefs of Christians.

The Rise of Apologetics

The practice of *apologetics* is considered a legitimate Christian discipline, taking its cue from the words of Peter in 1 Peter 3:15, "*Be ready always to give an answer to every man that asketh you a reason of the hope that is within you with meekness and fear.*" Perhaps the most celebrated apologist of the post-apostolic age was a man named Justin.

Justin Martyr, as he is now called, was born in approximately A.D. 100. He died via martyrdom in *circa* 165 A.D. Justin embraced Christianity in A.D. 130. Later, he taught at Ephesus. He wrote his first apology in A.D. 155 and his second apology, addressed to the Roman senate, in approximately 161. Justin's writings aimed at convincing the authorities that Christians were not criminals.

Justin believed in the inspiration and divine authority of the Scriptures. He argued in his apologies that Christianity was superior to Greek philosophy. He wrote, "Our doctrines then appear to be greater than all human teaching. For whatever either lawgivers or philosophers uttered well, they elaborated by finding and contemplating some part of the word. But since they did not know the whole word, which is Christ, they often contradicted themselves."[2]

---

1 An apologist is one who defends the faith against detractors.

Justin argued that no one trusted in Socrates enough to die for him as they did for the teachings of Jesus Christ. Justin Martyr also recorded orthodox views on the resurrection of the body. He said, "We expect to receive again our own bodies, though they be dead and cast into the earth, for we maintain that with God nothing is impossible."[3]

One of the most celebrated portions of Justin's writing is his detailed description of early Christian worship. He wrote,

> On the day called Sunday, there is a gathering together in the same place of all who live in a given city or rural district. The memoirs of the apostles [by which he has reference to the four Gospels, or the writings of the prophets] are read as long as time permits. Then when the reader ceases, the president, in a discourse, admonishes and urges the imitation of these good things. Next, we all rise together and send up prayers. When we cease from our prayer, bread is presented and wine and water. The president, in the same manner, sends up prayers and thanksgivings according to his ability, and the people sing out their assent, saying the 'Amen'. A distribution and participation of the elements, for which thanks have been given, is made to each person, and to those who are not present, they are sent by the deacons. Those who have means and are willing, each according to his own choice, gives what he wills, and what is collected is deposited with the president. He provides for the orphans and widows, those who are in need on account of sickness or some other cause, those who are in bonds, strangers who are sojourning, and in a word, he becomes the protector of all who are in need.[4]

---

2 Norman Geisler, *Baker Encyclopedia of Christian Apologetics*, "Justin Martyr," p. 395.

3 Ibid. p. 396.

4 Justin, "The First Apology," Ch. 67.

Justin's ministry took him eventually to Rome where he engaged in public debate with two philosophers, Marcion, known to be a heretic, and Crescens, a cynic. Legend has it that Crescens, stinging from his defeat in debate, reported Justin and six of his students to Rusticus, the prefect of Rome. In an A.D. 165 account of the trial, Rusticus questioned Justin and the others about their beliefs. Justin gave a short summary of Christian doctrine, and the others all confessed to being Christians. The prefect then asked him to denounce his faith by making a sacrifice to the gods. Justin replied, "No one who is rightly minded turns from true belief to false."

At the conclusion of his trial, the prefect sentenced Justin to death by beheading in A.D. 165 because he chose Christ over the Roman gods. He is remembered in Christian history to this day as Justin Martyr.

5
The Age of Doctrinal Confusion
A.D. 200 - 600

The 3rd and 4th centuries of church history were characterized by a struggle to maintain doctrinal purity in the wake of an influx of numerous heresies and theological aberrations. If the persecutions of the 2nd century constituted Satan's attack from without, the various heresies of the next few centuries constituted his attack from within.

The deviations in doctrine were centered around three primary areas: Christology (the doctrine of Christ's person & work), Ecclesiology (the doctrine of the nature, polity and function of the church), and Soteriology (the doctrine of salvation). Because some people find discussions about controversy unpalatable, they tend to pay little attention to this particular era in church history; however, neglecting this era will prove to be a serious mistake, for nothing is more beneficial to an understanding of the current landscape of the Christian community, and nothing more conducive to an ability to interpret subsequent historical events, than a grasp of the issues during this period in Christian history.

For instance, have you ever wondered where "Christian Scientism," "Unitarianism," "the Jesus Seminar," the New Age Movement and other eastern-oriented traditions that blend mysticism and Christianity originated? How about Catholicism's claim to be the true church? When did the idea of the church as a magisterial and redemptive institution consisting of both state and people, instead of a simple gathering of regenerate believers with a ministerial purpose and objective, originate? And why do some people teach that sinners are saved by God's free grace while others teach that salvation is by man's free will? The answer to each of these questions is rooted in an understanding of this era in church history.

It has been said that controversy tends to refine theological precision. Though unpleasant, the doctrinal challenges encountered during this era forced the church to clarify and codify certain key doctrines.

It might be argued by those of a more ecumenical mindset that because the various conflicts led to numerical division, those that insisted on identifying the errors and labored to refute them were in the wrong. But in New Testament terms, controversy over material doctrine simply distinguishes between true believers and unbelievers. Both Paul and John speak of how doctrinal controversy tends to separate authentic believers from spurious: "*But there must be heresies among you, that they which are approved may be made manifest*" (1 Cor. 11:19; cf. 1 Jno. 2:19).

The commitment of many brave servants of Christ during this era indicates that they believed that truth matters and that the essential truths of the Christian faith must be defended against human error. Though the World Council of Churches would later adopt as their motto the mantra "Doctrine divides, but service unites," yet many generations following the faithful men of the early church, including our own, owe a debt of gratitude to those who fought the good fight of faith and earnestly contended for the faith which was once delivered to the saints. Had they refused the call to rise to the challenges of their time, the errors of men may well have eclipsed the true gospel of Jesus Christ.

Christology

The initial deviation to orthodoxy concerned the area of Christology, or the doctrine of Christ's person and work. The first of these, and the mother of all the rest, was an error called ***Gnosticism,*** or the Secret Knowledge Movement.

It is generally agreed that the seeds of third-century *Gnosticism* within the Christian community were sown in the 1st century. The epistles of *Colossians* and *1 John* suggest that the church was troubled by *Gnostic* influence as early as the middle of the first century.

Since the discovery of manuscripts at Nag Hammadi in 1946, the basic tenets of *Gnostic* theology are now indisputable. This distortion was actually a blend of Greek mystery religion, Persian and Oriental mysticism, and Christianity. It posited a dualistic view of good and evil, light and darkness, spirit and matter. *Gnostics* (derived from the Greek word *gnosis*, or "knowledge") believed that the material world was evil and that only secret, existential knowledge could liberate people from the bondage of the physical world. *Gnostics* were, consequently, anti-institutional. They favored nature sanctuaries over artificial houses of worship and mystical experience over God's special revelation in Scripture.

It was in terms of the doctrine of Christ, however, that *Gnosticism* posed a formidable threat to the integrity of the Christian faith. Contrary to John 1:14, the *Gnostics* did not believe that Christ became flesh. They taught that Christ was a spirit that temporarily possessed an ordinary human being named Jesus. John's warning about the spirit of antichrist that denies that "*Jesus Christ is come in the flesh*" (1 Jno. 4:2-3) is direct apologetic thrust against *Gnosticism*.

One of the most influential of the early *Gnostics* was a man named Marcion. He migrated to the city of Rome where he developed his ideas and built a significant following. According to Marcion, Christ was a spirit and only seemed human. This belief would later become known as ***Docetism***. The church at Rome eventually excluded Marcion for heresy, but he went on to establish his own congregations in Italy and Asia Minor.

In A.D. 205, Origen of Alexandria began to espouse various *Gnostic* ideas. He taught that God's original creation was spiritual and only after the Fall did He form a physical world. He insisted that the Bible contained many hidden, mystic messages and that people should seek this secret knowledge. He renounced all physical comforts, drank only water, wore no shoes, and made himself a eunuch. Because of his influence and the seeds of *Gnosticism* he had sown, many Christians renounced physical pleasure for lifelong celibacy and retreated to solitude to seek salvation via mysticism. So, the roots of monasticism and ascetism began to grow in the soil of *Gnostic* ideas.

To counter the growing *Gnostic* crisis, Christians sought to assemble a canon (the word means "rule" or "measuring stick") for faith and life. There were *Gnostic* writings aplenty, such as the "Text without Title" on the origin of the world. There were also Gospels and Epistles that had been circulated among the churches for the past century and a half. The question "On which writings should God's people rely?" left Christian people in a quandry.

To determine which writings should be included in the canon of inspired Scripture, Christian people asked three basic questions:

1. Is the writing of apostolic origin?

2. Is the writing categorically accepted and used by the churches?
3. Is the writing consistent with what the Old Testament reveals about God?

Though debates continued over a few books such as *Hebrews, James,* and *2 Peter,* yet by the 3rd century Christian people had reached consensus about the basic canon of New Testament Scripture. The *Gnostic* writings were categorically rejected by the churches because they did not satisfy the three basic criteria of apostolicity, comprehensive use and accceptance, and consistency with Old Testament revelation. From this point forward, orthodoxy would be determined by the benchmark of the New Testament canon alone.

Ecclesiology

Christians in Rome also attempted to counter the raging doctrinal confusion by investing more power in the overseers of the church. These bishops, viewed as successors to the apostles, became the official trustees of apostolic teaching. One historian writes, "In larger cities, their powers expanded rapidly. Since city overseers nurtured God's children throughout entire regions, they began calling one another 'popes'—Latin for 'fathers'...A priesthood of church leaders was replacing the priesthood of all believers."[1] Monasticism was gaining a stronghold in the organized church.

When Constantine became Roman Emperor in 311 A.D., he initially practiced a policy of toleration toward Christians. Soon, he claimed conversion and began to defend the Christian faith. Under his oversight, Bishops began to receive liberal salaries from the

1 Dr. Timothy Paul Jones, *Christian History Made Easy,* p. 22.

State and were made rulers of large cities. They lived in luxury. The original simplicity of the church was gradually being replaced by pomp and ceremony. The church began to operate more like a large organization or institution with a hierarchical structure, instead of the body of Christ. It wasn't long before Constantine assumed ultimate power as the "head of the church."

All the while, some continued to worship according to the primitive pattern, increasingly deciding to stand aloof from these aberrations. The dynamic of Christian churches distancing themselves from the radical changes taking place is termed in scholastic circles of Christian history "the Free Church movement."

One author writes, "The process of development which transformed the original Christian congregations to a sacramental, authoritarian Church took place during the latter portion of the second century...This change did not take place without protest... Many church historians have dismissed as heretics those churches that opposed the institutionalized church—a campaign often called 'The Free Church Movement"[2]

Dr. James Stitzinger writes about these groups who refused to be amalgamated into what was becoming Roman Catholicism, "A thorough investigation of these independents is difficult, because, for the most part, only the works of those who wrote against them have survived...Such groups include the Montanists (ca. A. D. 156), Novatians (ca. A. D. 250), and Donatists (ca. A. D. 311), all of whom left the official church of their day to pursue the pure church."[3]

---

[2] Gunnar Westin, *The Free Church through the Ages*, p. 9.

[3] James Stitzinger, *Rediscovering Pastoral Ministry*, "Pastoral Ministry in History," p. 45.

The relationship between Constantine and the Donatists was not pleasant. In his *History of the Christian Church,* Philip Schaff comments about what is termed “the Donatist Controversy”:

> The Donatist controversy was a conflict between separatism and Catholicism; between ecclesiastical purism and ecclesiastical eclecticism; between the idea of the church as an exclusive community of regenerated saints and the idea of the church as the general Christendom of state and people.[4]

Several points are noteworthy in Schaff’s explanation. The Donatists were concerned with the purity of the church. They wanted to conduct church life and worship according to the apostolic pattern. Constantine, on the other hand, wanted to redefine the Church as an “eclectic” or “all-inclusive” institution. The Donatists believed in a regenerated church membership. No one but believers who gave evidence of being born again would be admitted into the membership of the church. Constantine, on the other hand, believed that the church and state should be indistinguishable – that the church included everyone everywhere—a “catholic” or universal demographic.

This movement from the simplicity of apostolic Christianity to the complexity of institutionalism was the beginning of sorrows—the tip of the iceberg of apostasy. Understanding the circumstances of this polarizing period is critical to a proper interpretation of church history.

---

4 Philip Schaff, *History of the Christian Church*, pp 365-366.

Arianism & the Council of Nicea

Perhaps the most significant challenge to the doctrine of Christ's person came in the latter half of the 3rd century and first half of the 4th. A bishop from Alexandria, Egypt named Arius began to teach that Jesus was not God, but was the first and highest created being.[5] He set his message to a catchy jingle and soon people were singing in the streets, "Once the Son did not exist."

Another Alexandrian, a theologian named Athanasius, countered Arius with a book entitled *On the Incarnation of the Word of God* and heated debate between the two sides was the result. It is highly doubtful that Constantine cared about the deity of Christ,[6] but he did care about the unity of the Empire. He arranged a council at Nicaea (a city about 30 miles southeast of Constantinople, or modern Istanbul) on July 4, 325 A.D.

The question to be decided was this: "Is the Son of God of the same substance as the Father, or of similar substance?" Athanasius insisted on the former; Arius on the latter.

Record indicates that 318 bishops were present. At first, one group stridently disagreed with Arius, while another supported him. The majority only wanted peace and thought the debate over the Greek words *similar* and *same* was immaterial. But when one of Arius' supporters took it upon himself to explain the Arian position, bedlam erupted and the Council condemned the idea that Christ was created as blasphemy.

An elder from Asia Minor named Marcellus suggested that the delegates use the Greek word Athanasius used to describe the person of Christ—i.e. *homoousios*, meaning "one and the same"—instead

---

5 This view is echoed by modern-day Jehovah's Witnesses.

6 In fact, Constantine gave the opening speech at the Council stating that doctrinal disunity was worse than war.

of *homoiousios*, the word Arius preferred, a word that added an extra letter (i.e. the letter "i"). By a vote of 316 to 2, the Council adopted what has come to be known as the Nicene Creed, which declares Jesus Christ to be *"very God of very God...being of one substance with the Father, by whom all things were made."* When Bible students today say that Christ is "co-substantial" and "co-essential" with the Father, they are taking a stand for Christian orthodoxy against the Arian heresy.

This was a defining moment in Christian history, for it codified the important doctrine of Christ's deity and protected it against maverick interpretations. Some scholars have ridiculed the fact that the council split over one "*iota*." The difference between the Greek word for *similar* (Arius' position) and the word for *same* (Athanasius' position) is a single letter—i.e. the letter *i*. They claim it is just like theologians to debate trivial matters while neglecting the real-life problems that people face.

But Dr. Erwin Lutzer, pastor of Moody Church in Chicago, however, posits an answer to this objection, by repeating a story that demonstrates how a single letter, or mark of punctuation, can change the entire meaning of a message. He writes:

> "Back in the days when messages were sent by telegraph there was a code for each punctuation mark. A woman touring Europe cabled her husband to ask whether she could buy a beautiful bracelet for $75,000. The husband sent this message back: "No, price too high." The cable operator, however, in transmitting the message, missed the signal for the comma. The woman received the message "No price too high." She bought the bracelet. The husband subsequently

> sued the company and won! After that, people using Morse code observed the habit of spelling out every mark of punctuation. Clearly, a comma or an 'iota' can make a big difference when communicating a message!"

Of course, the Council of Nicaea did not invent the doctrine of Christ's Deity, any more than Sir Isaac Newton invented the law of gravity. They merely recognized and affirmed a doctrine that had been believed by Christians long before this group of 300+ bishops met.

For example, Pliny's letter to the Emperor Trajan, dated *circa* A.D. 107, speaks of Christians joining "together in singing hymns to Christ as to a deity."[7] In A.D. 110, Ignatius, bishop of Antioch, wrote, "There is One God who manifests himself through Jesus Christ his Son." And Polycarp, bishop of Smyrna, sent an epistle to the church at Philippi, *circa* A.D. 112-118, in which he assumes that those to whom it is addressed "acknowledge the divinity of Jesus, his exaltation to heaven, and his subsequent glorification." Each of these extra-Biblical references appears two centuries before the Council of Nicaea convened.

Subsequent quotes from Justin Martyr (*circa* A.D. 150), who called Christ "the son and apostle of God the Father and master of all," Irenaeus (*circa* A.D. 177), who speaking of John 1:1 stated that "all distinctions between the Father and the Son vanish, for the one God made all things through His word," and Tertullian (*circa* A.D. 200), who affirmed both a fully divine and fully human Christ, appear in the annals of history prior to Nicaea, and stand as evidence

7 C. B. & Sylvester Hassell, *History of the Church of God*, p. 359.

that the consensus of the primitive church was that Jesus Christ was the eternal Son of God.

An orthodox Christology has historically been defined by a Trinitarian formula that neither divides the Nature nor confounds the Persons of the Godhead. Nicaea survives as the most popular statement of that formula. We may be certain, however, that though no official documentation survives, those detractors of Constantine whose passion it was to pursue a pure church according to the apostolic pattern also maintained a doctrine of Christ that affirmed both his Divine and his human natures.

Soteriology

It was also during this period that disputes arose concerning the doctrine of salvation. There are two primary soteriological developments during this era that are significant in Christian history.

The first is Cyprian's famous dictum, *Extra ecclesium nulla salus* – "There is no salvation outside the church." Cyprian ministered in Carthage in approximately 255 A.D. This well-known sentence expresses the idea that the "church," through Word and Sacrament, mediates—as the means or instrument—God's grace in salvation.

Cyprian of Carthage

Historically, the phrase "means of grace" (*media gratiae*) has been employed, both by sacerdotal traditions (such as Catholicism and Anglicanism) who emphasize the Sacramental acts as more or less salvific, and evangelical traditions (such as Lutheranism, Presbyterianism, and other Reformed traditions) who emphasize the preaching of the Word as the instrument of salvation. Though debate continues between the two schools of thought over which *media* should have priority—i.e. the Word or the Sacraments—yet both share a common conviction that salvation is mediated through the "church," without which, there is no salvation. *Extra ecclesiam nulla salus*.

But is that fundamental assumption correct? Is the "church" a redemptive institution? In a word, did God make the equation of grace contingent on the variable of human instrumentality? Many Christian denominations today say "yes."

Primitive Baptists believe, however, that the church is a pastoral (i.e. with respect to discipleship and the care of the flock), not a redemptive (i.e. with respect to eternal salvation) institution. Jesus Christ himself, not the church, is the "*one Mediator between God and men*" (1 Tim. 2:5)—the only means by which the salvific benefits of the covenant of redemption are dispensed. Neither the preached word or the ordinances of the church have any role in eternal salvation, but are intended for the education, encouragement, and edification of believers in this world.

This distinction between those who have adopted Cyprian's dictum and those who insist that Jesus Christ alone is the Mediator (or means) of salvation is the primary difference between Primitive Baptists and other Christian traditions today. Most groups affirm Cyprian's formula as axiomatic. Primitive Baptists, however, deny that the church exists to help the Lord populate heaven. Instead, the church exists to "*teach*" (or disciple) baptized believers "*to observe all things that* [Christ] *has commanded*" (cf. Mt. 28:18-19) and to "*feed*" (or tend as a shepherd) "*the church* [Christ] *has purchased with His own blood*" (cf. Acts 20:28).

The second episode of note was a debate in *circa* 420 A.D. between two monks, Augustine of Hippo (in North Africa) and

Augustine of Hippo

Pelagius, a pious British monk. Pelagius denied original sin, insisting that Adam's sin did not affect the entire human race. At birth, he said, people are able to do everything that God requires of them if they will only exercise the human will. The ability to be saved is resident in the heart of man, he taught.

When his teachings reached Hippo, Augustine wasted no time. He countered Pelagianism in a work entitled *Contra Duas Epistulas Pelagianorum.* He argued from Paul's letters that Adam's original sin corrupted all humanity and that this corruption is so extensive and radical that no one is naturally inclined toward God. He insisted that salvation must be by grace alone, not by man's free-will, due to the fact of man's inherent depravity.

Of course, Augustine broke from Pauline theology when he argued (according to Cyprian's idea discussed previously) that the rite of infant baptism would purify a person from inherent sin. He believed, like virtually all of his contemporaries, that saving grace would be mediated through the church.

Nevertheless, this titanic struggle between the idea of salvation by God's free grace and of salvation by man's free-will would set the theological pace for years to come. Even today, some Christian people insist on a modified version of Pelagianism, saying that man is not *totally* depraved and can, therefore, save himself by some good work or some decision that he makes. Others, taking their cue from Augustine, believed that man is hopelessly ruined because of sin. The only hope of salvation is an alien (i.e. something outside of himself) righteousness accounted to the account, and a vital holiness created in the heart of a person by the grace of God alone.

The Novatians

A discussion of this turbulent period in Christian history would not be complete without a more specific look at those groups that conscientiously objected to the changes that were taking place under Constantine. As previously noted, documentation of groups in the "free church" tradition is comparatively scant because only the works of those who wrote against them have survived. Some material is available, however, on the Novatians or Cathari ("the Pure").

The Primitive Baptist historians C. B. and Sylvester Hassell write, "Novatian was a very learned and upright elder in the church at Rome."[8] When in 251 A.D., another elder named Cornelius wanted to readmit people who had lapsed during the Decian persecution, Novatian opposed such laxity in discipline on the grounds that the church should be a communion of saints. Cornelius, the loose disciplinarian, prevailed, and Novatian and the minority withdrew from the majority to pursue the pure church.

Hassell states, "There can be no question that these were Baptist churches...They would receive no members from such loose societies except by rebaptizing them."[9] He emphasizes that the initial separation was caused by a difference in discipline, not because of a difference in doctrine.

After the Council of Nicaea in A.D. 325, Constantine wrote letters enjoining universal conformity to its decrees. Soon, he issued edicts against maverick groups he deemed to be heretics, whom he

---

8 Hassell, *History of the Church of God,* p. 377.

9 Ibid.

deprived of the liberty of meeting for worship either in public or private places. The Novatians were among those he targeted. These penal laws "obliged them to lurk in corners and worship God in private."[10]

The Novatians were criticized for their strict gospel discipline as well as for their refusal to revere the martyrs and ascribe virtue to their relics. Though Constantine labeled them as heretics, it is clear that their doctrine was very scriptural. Novatian himself wrote a work on the subject of the Trinity that is still extant. The heretical charge (it seems clear) was primarily due to their refusal to participate in what they believed to be ecclesiastical corruptions.

The Donatists

Another group vilified as heretics were the Donatists, *circa* 411 A.D. Donatus fell into disfavor with Constantine when he protested the marriage of church and state. Donatus asked, "What has the emperor to do with the church?"

When Constantine granted religious toleration to Christians in the Edict of Milan, A.D. 312, he particularly made an exception for the Donatists. Tolerance did not apply to them. In response, the Donatists appealed to the emperor to examine their doctrinal principles. Constantine responded by appointing a council of 20 bishops to do so in 313 A.D., and another council of 200 in August of 314 A.D. He even granted them a personal audience at Milan in 316. Each time, however, the Donatists were condemned and labeled as rebels and schismatics for resisting the authority of the emperor.

Edicts were issued to confiscate their property and deprive them of their church buildings. Other royal edicts sentenced them to banishment, and even death. Hassell indicates that the Donatists

10 Hassell, p. 387.

"advocated the purity and unworldliness of the church and the necessity of strict discipline; like the Montanists and the Novatians, the Donatists baptized all whom they received into their churches, whether such had previously been allegedly baptized or not. Their churches were independent of each other in government."[11]

In 411 A.D., Augustine argued that the state had the responsibility to use force to bring the Donatists into conformity to Catholicism, but other political developments terminated the proposal before it could be executed.

To this day, most historians refer to the Donatists as "heretics," but it is evident that the issue of perspective is always relevant when charging someone with being a heretic. Any real and documented evidence that the Donatists were anything but sincere believers in apostolic Christianity is conspicuous by its absence.

More could be said of those who conscientiously objected to the reforms being perpetrated on the church during the post-apostolic era. There were numerous other small, splinter groups that refused to participate in what appeared to be deviations from biblical criteria—groups committed to the "pursuit of the true church or 'primitivism'"[12] and a return to the original, apostolic pattern, including Tertullian, the Montanists, Paulicians, Waldenses, and others who withdrew from the increasingly institutionalized church because of its corruptions. Indeed, these groups had their own alleged eccentricities, albeit the accuracy of these "hearsay" allegations is suspect in lieu of the lack of evidence.[13] But this is

11 Hassell, p. 390.

12 Stitzinger, Rediscovering Pastoral Ministry, "Pastoral Ministry in History," p. 35.

13 Most of their own literature was destroyed by their persecutors. Since "history is written by the winners," reports that they were unorthodox is likely exaggerated. Of course, extremes here and there are plausible, but it is also

sufficient to establish the point that Catholicism was not the only option. It is my studied opinion, moreover, that it was by means of these various "free church" groups—groups that were viewed as nonconformists and rebels—that Christ preserved his church during this period of doctrinal confusion and deviation from the New Testament pattern of doctrine and worship.

---

possible that "talking points" such as the popular opinion that the Montanists favored mysticism may simply be a reaction to their rejection of a growing emphasis on external rites and forms within Catholicism.

PART 3

The Medieval Period

A.D. 600 - 1500

6
The Dark Ages
A.D. 600 - 1500

The period between A.D. 600 and 1500 in Christian history is called the Middle, or Dark, Ages. It covers a period of approximately 900 years between A.D. 600 and 1500. It is called "dark" because the light of truth was largely obscured, both in terms of secular culture and of religious liberty.

In secular terms, the Dark Ages refers to the post-Roman Empire culture between the declining influence of ancient Rome and the Italian Renaissance, and it describes the cultural and economic decline that occurred in Western Europe during that period. Religiously speaking, the Dark Ages was a time of pervasive superstition.

Very little historical information is available from this era beyond what is available through Roman Catholic sources. This was the era of the Crusades, superstition, and general ignorance. European legends such as Robin Hood and King Arthur originated during the feudal system of government that was practiced during this era. Few people could read, and Catholic priests turned to images, icons, architecture, stories, statues, and rituals to teach the common people about God.

The Birth of Islam and Its Relation to Christianity

While superstition was taking root in the West, Islam, a new and rival world religion, was growing in the East. Never has Christianity had a greater foe than the religion of Islam.

The Muslim religion originated in approximately 600 A.D. Mohammad, the founder, was born in Mecca of Arabia in 470 A.D. Orphaned as a little child, he was raised by his uncle Abu Talib, who exposed him to various Jewish and Christian settlements as he traveled with him on business. He was troubled, however, by the proliferation of images and icons associated with these religions, adjudging them to be forms of idolatry.

At the age of 25, Mohammad entered the service of a wealthy widow to carry on her husband's trade. He married the widow who was fourteen years his senior, and successfully managed her late husband's business. Over the next decade or so, he grew more serious about religion until at the age of 40, Mohammad spent an entire month in solitude in a mountain cave near Mecca.

He claimed that he received the following message in a vision from the angel Gabriel: "O, Mohammad, of a truth thou art the prophet of God. Fear not. I am his angel Gabriel." Mohammad called his new religion *Islam*, meaning "submission." He recognized that Moses and Jesus were prophets, but claimed that he was the greatest prophet of all. Mohammad emerged from solitude and began to challenge the idolatry around him.

Mohammad, however, was not initially received with enthusiasm. In 622, he and his followers were forced to flee to Medina for their safety. Eight years later, he returned to Mecca in triumph and destroyed over 300 idols in the city. Overwhelmed by this dramatic turn of events, the city's inhabitants shouted, "There is but one god, Allah, and Mohammad is his prophet."

Mohammad's new religion had great appeal to his fellow Arabians. Over a twenty-three year period, Mohammad collected the "divine secrets" that had been allegedly revealed to him in a book called the *Quran,* the greatest masterpiece in Arabic literature. The *Quran* furnishes Muslims with most of their prayers and permits the followers of Islam to have as many as four wives each.

Mohammad taught that God has historically sent different prophets to reveal his various attributes—Moses, his providence and mercy; Solomon, his wisdom, majesty, and glory; Jesus, his righteousness, omniscience, and power. "But I, the last of the prophets," said Mohammed, "am sent with the sword."

He taught, "Let those who promulgate my faith enter into no argument or discussion, but slay all who refuse obedience to the law. Whoever fights for the true faith, whether he fall or conquer, will assuredly receive a glorious reward and be certain of entrance into paradise. Prayer leads halfway to God. Fasting leads to the gateway to heaven. Alms opens the door, but waging the holy war gives actual entrance in heaven."[1]

Islam teaches that everything that happens has been foreordained by an absolute fate, and that after death, the evil will be punished and the good rewarded. The five pillars of Islam are: 1. The confession of no other god but Allah; 2. The offering up of prayers five times each day; 3. The giving of alms; 4. Fasting during daylight hours throughout the entire month of Ramadan; 5. Pilgrimage to Mecca at least once in a person's lifetime.

After his conquest of Mecca, Mohammad demanded recognition as the messenger of God from emperors and kings. After his death in 632, his followers known as the *Caliphs*

---

1 S. M. Houghton, *Sketches from Church History,* p. 36.

founded the Muslim empire, which stretched from India to the Atlantic Ocean. In 637, Caliph Omar seized control of Jerusalem and built a mosque on the site of the old Jewish temple. Later, he burned the world's most famous library located in Alexandria, Egypt. He justified the unconscionable act saying that the *Quran* was the only book necessary.

By 662, Islam had established a dominant presence in Syria, Egypt, Mesopotamia, Persia, and North Africa. Thousands of Christian churches were destroyed or converted into mosques. In the 700's, Muslims infiltrated Europe via Spain and France, sustaining a strong presence in the former for over 700 years.

Islam is the only world religion to be established since the coming of Jesus Christ into the world. Like Christianity, it is a monotheistic religion. And again, like the Christian faith, it is an exclusive faith.

Today, exclusivity is taboo. Any religion that claims to be absolutely true is viewed by the secular culture as intolerant. Hence, neither Christianity nor Islam is popularly accepted by the world. Moreover, mutually exclusive religions such as Christianity and Islam cannot tolerate each other. If the intolerance were strictly academic, however, the two major world religions could peacefully coexist. When one or the other party addresses the dilemma politically and militantly, however—as Catholicism regrettably did in the Crusades and Islam is doing today—the prospect for the future looks very tenuous and bleak.

The Crusades

The rapid growth of Islam was causing great concern in papal Rome. The Muslims had controlled Jerusalem since A.D. 638. Pilgrims to Jerusalem were allowed to visit but not permitted to publicly demonstrate in favor of Christianity or to build any churches. In the 11th century, however, Christian pilgrims to Jerusalem were subjected to high tariffs, harsh treatment, and severe oppression.

In 1095, Pope Urban II delivered a homily against the Turks and Arabs, urging Catholics to "destroy that vile race from their lands." He probably did not anticipate the effect his sermon would have on his people. A cry went up that the Turks should be dislodged by force. "It is the will of God. It is the will of God," exclaimed the people.

Peter the Hermit rode his donkey from city to city throughout Italy and France preaching against the oppressors of the pilgrims. He gathered an army of 20,000 European peasants who affixed a red cross to their right shoulder as a badge of honor.

These uncouth peasants were long on enthusiasm and short on training for warfare. The Turks met them at Nicaea (just south of Constantinople) and killed most of them. Four years later, another group of "Christian" crusaders, now trained in warfare, recaptured Nicaea, then captured Antioch of Syria, and proceeded to take Jerusalem in a gruesome massacre of nearly all the Turks in the city. For nearly fifty years, Jerusalem remained under Catholic control, but it was under constant threat by the followers of Mohammad. This was the First Crusade.

In 1147, Bernard of Clairvaux, a pious monk and writer of Christian hymns, preached about the need for a Second Crusade to support the kingdom of Jerusalem. Two substantial armies were gathered, one led by the king of France and the other by the emperor of Germany. As the armies marched for Jerusalem, however, they suffered severe casualties at the hands of the Turks, again in Nicaea. The armies retreated homeward, and the

Muslims, now encouraged by their success, laid siege to Jerusalem and recaptured it in the fall of 1147.

The Europeans were indignant. This time Richard the Lionheart, king of England, joined Barbarossa of Germany and Philip Augustus, king of France, on the Third Crusade. Only Richard, however, would reach Jerusalem.[2] The German emperor was drowned while attempting to cross a river in Asia Minor. The king of France returned home after illness weakened his ranks. Knowing that he could not take Jerusalem alone, Richard negotiated the terms of a truce with the Muslim leader Saladin. Saladin agreed that Christian pilgrims to the city would no longer be molested or taxed. Richard, then, boarded a ship and headed home for England.

At least four other crusades were attempted, none of which were successful in conquering the Muslims. The Fourth Crusade saw European Catholics distracted into fighting their eastern brothers in Constantinople. For three days, the Crusaders sacked Constantinople. One eastern writer lamented, "Muslims are merciful compared with these men who bear Christ's cross on their shoulders." It was this crusade that forever divided Catholicism into two groups—Roman Catholic and Eastern Orthodox.

Not every feature of the two hundred years of Crusades was a violation of Christian principles. Even some secular critics of Christianity recognize that the Crusaders constructed hospitals in Palestine and other parts of the Middle East during this sad period. These nobler acts notwithstanding, the Crusades left a

---

2 The Robin Hood legends, by the way, supposedly took place while Richard was gone on this Third Crusade.

blemish on Christianity's reputation in the world—one that has diminished very little over time.

Jesus taught that because his kingdom was not of this world, it would not be promoted by the use of the sword (Jno. 18:36; Mt. 26:52). Paul reminded the Corinthians that "*the weapons of our warfare are not carnal, but mighty through God to the pulling down of strongholds*" (2 Cor. 10:4). The cause of Christ would have been much better served had his professed followers always remembered that basic principle.

PART 4

The Age of Reformation

A.D. 1500 - 1600

7
Pre-Reformation Lights
A.D. 1300 - 1500

In his book *Sketches from Church History,* S. M. Houghton refers to the institutionalized "Church" (or Roman Catholicism) when he says,

> The condition of the church in the Middle Ages was pitiful. The masses of the people had a blind faith in the doctrines and traditions of the church and never inquired whether they were in harmony with the scriptures. If you could read, books were scarce. It was a rare thing for a man to have any real acquaintance with the word of God. Superstition increased alarmingly. The doctrine of indulgences gained general acceptance. The church taught that forgiveness of sins might be obtained by the rendering of service to the church, and in the thirteenth century, indulgences were even sold for money.[1]

This was truly a time of gross spiritual darkness, but the sunbeams of truth were not totally eclipsed by Catholicism. A group in the valleys of the Swiss Piedmont and in southern France known as the Waldensians, or "the poor men of Lyons," had gospel light in their dwellings.

---

1 S. M. Houghton, *Sketches from Church History,* pp. 59-60.

The Waldensian Seal

The Waldensian Seal employs the motto *Lux Lucet in Tenebris*, meaning "Light Shineth in Darkness." Later, the Protestant Reformers would claim the motto *Post Tenebras Lux* ("After Darkness, Light"). Indeed, Luther, Calvin, Zwingli, Knox and the other Reformers would bring a certain light of truth after the darkness of medieval superstition and ignorance, but the preponderance of evidence throughout Christian history affirms that the light of truth was never totally extinguished. It is a fact recognized by very few historians that light shined even in the darkness of the Middle Ages, for numerous "free church" groups that pursued what some historians have termed "the Believer's Church" and practiced a commitment to "primitivism" have maintained a witness and a testimony to apostolic Christianity in every age.[2]

Permit me to state it another way. Popular historians tend to categorize the Waldenses, Lollards and Hussites as "forerunners of the Reformation," i.e. groups that paved the way for Luther,

2 In James F. Stitzinger, "Pastoral Ministry in History," p.35 in *Rediscovering Pastoral Ministry* (Word Publishing, 1995), the author writes: "In every generation some have sought to return to the basic fundamentals of primitive biblical ministry. This pursuit of the true church or 'primitivism' has led Littell and others to speak of the concept of the 'Believer's Church'."

Calvin and the rest to rediscover Christianity after it was lost in the Dark Ages. Those of us in Baptist schools of thought, however, affirm that "*the faith*" (that is, the body of revealed truth) was "*once*[3] *delivered to the saints*" (cf. Jude 3); therefore, we see these groups as evidence, not that truth was totally lost and later reclaimed but rather, that the light of truth was never completely extinguished from the earth. It appears that the best way to say it is that even though it was partially eclipsed, the light still shined in the midst of the Dark Ages. It didn't have to be rekindled after the Dark Ages.

Ephesians 3:21 indicates that the Lord Jesus Christ will be glorified in his church "*throughout all ages, world without end,*" not that he will receive glory for a few centuries, followed by a void of silence, and then finally be glorified again when the Protestant Reformers rediscover the gospel. Indeed, through these nonconformist groups (that we Baptists, due to so many parallels with their convictions, claim as our ancestors), the light of truth continued to shine in the midst of the darkness. One such notable group was the Waldenses, or as some refer to them, the Waldensians.

Those Incorrigible Waldenses

The Waldenses, named for their founder Peter Waldo, emphasized the Scripture alone as the basis of faith, and insisted that Christ is the one and only mediator between God and men (1 Tim. 2:5). They rejected the worship of "saints" and, in contrast to Catholicism which observed seven sacraments, only observed two ordinances—baptism by immersion and the Lord's Supper.

---

3 The Greek word means "once for all."

The Waldenses were very evangelistic. They mobilized in groups of two, disguising themselves as peddlers trying to sell knick-knacks. Whenever they found a listening ear, they proclaimed God's word fearlessly, criticizing the false teachings and traditions of Catholicism. The growing momentum and popularity of these lay ministers soon drew the ire of authorities. They were condemned as heretics at the 3rd and 4th Lateran Councils, and those who were not "priests" were forbidden to read the Bible. The Bible was placed on the "Index of Forbidden Books."

When the Waldensians refused to curtail their activities, prosecution resulted. Inquisitors hunted the simple and pious Waldenses for many years. Thousands were slain in the Piedmont. Mothers with infants were rolled down the rocks. As persecution intensified, the Waldenses fled to the mountains for safety. "At one time, 400 women and children were housed in a cave while the men were away. When this hiding place was discovered, the enemies lit a fire at the opening of the cave, and all who were within perished."[4] Persecution and martyrdom of the Waldenses continued until Oliver Cromwell declared, in 1655, "a solemn fast" on behalf of the sufferers and threatened to defend them with the British military.

The inquisitors could not deny, however, the purity of their morals and the sincerity of their convictions. Like their contemporaries, the Albigenses, the Waldenses were "the earliest champions...of our modern liberty of thought."[5] They were

---

4 Ibid. p. 63.

5 C. B. & S. Hassell, *History of the Church of God*, p. 438.

viewed as rebels because they refused to comply with papal corruptions and practiced anti-sacerdotalism.[6]

Elder Sylvester Hassell writes of the Waldenses that "they were very industrious, honest, modest, frugal, chaste, and temperate...they rejected the authority of the 'fathers' and the Catholic traditions, and the doctrines of purgatory, indulgences, transubstantiation, monasticism, sacramentalism, and celibacy."[7] Though their doctrinal purity in the 12th and 13th centuries was suspect—being more interested in the practical Christianity of James than the doctrinal orthodoxy of Paul—yet the Waldenses taught that God alone can forgive sin and that every believer can approach God as a priest.

Hence, the Waldenses, together with the Albigenses and the Petrobrusians, stand as testimony to the fact that various nonconformist groups maintained a separate and distinct identity to Catholicism even in the Middle Ages. It was through these devout and simple Christians who were committed to following the apostolic pattern of church life revealed in the New Testament that Christ preserved his church during the Dark Ages.

John Wycliffe: Hero or Heretic?

Though the Middle Ages were days of pervasive spiritual darkness, the birth of John Wycliffe in England in 1330 signaled the dawning of a new day. Wycliffe is called "the Morningstar of the Reformation" and the opening salvos of the Protestant Reformation of the 16th century are credited to him.

---

6 Anti-sacerdotalism is the idea that the "sacraments" or ordinances are commemorative, not redemptive, ceremonies.

7 Hassell, p. 440.

He and his English followers, called Lollards, exercised great influence on the Bohemians and their leader, John Huss, whose teachings, in turn, exercised great influence on Martin Luther. One hundred fifty years after Wycliffe, Luther would be accused by the Pope at the imperial *Diet of Worms* of reviving the errors of Wycliffe and Huss.

Though Wycliffe was a Roman Catholic, he was very critical of the corruptions of the clergy. He wrote and preached clearly in the Middle English dialect of the common man instead of formal Latin, and his popularity among the populace grew apace. His followers, the Lollards, were numerous. One historian wrote, "They were everywhere; a man could scarcely meet two people on the road, but one of them was a disciple of Wycliffe."[8]

Perhaps the most famous Lollard was Sir John Oldcastle, who was martyred by hanging and burning in London in 1417. In his book, *Welsh Succession of Primitive Baptist Faith and Practice*, Elder Mike Ivey writes, "It is probable that Lord Oldcastle was an old Baptist minister. Davis notes the Baptists sometimes met in the chapel at Olchon Court where Oldcastle preached."[9]

Wycliffe spent many years of his life challenging Roman Catholic dogma, such as the doctrine of transubstantiation, Cyprian's doctrine that salvation is only attainable through the church, and the erroneous belief that forgiveness can be purchased through indulgences. He taught that "the true Church was composed of the 'congregation of the predestined' as the Body of Christ, which Wycliffe contrasted with the visible or Church Militant.[10] He rejected the "ultra-predestinarian views of

8 *Christian History Magazine*, Vol II, No. 2, Issue 3, 1983, p. 17.

9 *Welsh Succession of Primitive Baptist Faith & Practice*, Michael N. Ivey, 1994, p. 56.

10 *Christian History Magazine*, Vol II, No. 2, Issue 3, p. 12.

Bradwardine" and sought to retain some of man's freedom. Wycliffe rejected the view that if any man sins, God himself determines that man to the act.[11]

In 1382, Wycliffe decided that the best way to counter the excesses of Rome was to translate the entire Bible into English. Prior to this time, only the Clergy had access to the scriptures and that only in formal Latin. By making the scriptures available to the common man in his own vernacular, Wycliffe enabled people to search God's word for themselves. Wycliffe wrote, "The laity ought to understand the faith, and as doctrines of our faith are in the Scriptures, believers should have the Scriptures in a language which they fully understand."[12]

He wrote, "Holy Scripture is the preeminent authority for every Christian and the rule of faith and of all human perfection...It alone is the supreme law that is to rule Church, State, and Christian life, without human traditions and statutes." Wycliffe's five rules for studying the Bible included the following instructions: "Obtain a reliable text, understand the logic of Scripture, compare the parts of Scripture with one another, maintain an attitude of humble seeking, and receive the instruction of the Holy Spirit."[13]

In 1377, Pope Gregory XI issued five papal bulls condemning the work of John Wycliffe as heresy. The bulls called Wycliffe a "deadly pest" who if not "plucked up by the roots" would "infect multitudes." Wycliffe responded to the bulls with a personal protest to the Archbishop at Lambeth Palace in which he claimed

11 Ibid. p. 11.
12 Op cit. p. 26.
13 Op cit.

to be “a sound Christian” who had “followed the Sacred Scriptures.” He was never, however, excommunicated.

After Wycliffe's death in 1384, his followers continued his work, copying the Holy Scriptures and distributing them to the people. Some of the students who had studied under Wycliffe at Oxford carried his writings to Bohemia where John Hus awaited the next leg of this relay for truth.

Forty years after the death of Wycliffe, the Council of Constance burned John Hus at the stake and condemned the deceased Wycliffe on 260 counts. They ordered his writings to be burned and his remains exhumed, burned, and scattered in the river. Wycliffe’s remains were more easily dispensed of, however, than his teachings. One historian wrote, “They burned his bones to ashes and cast them into the Swift, a neighboring brook running hard by. Thus, the brook conveyed his ashes into Avon, Avon into Severn, Severn into the narrow seas, and they into the main ocean. And thus, the Ashes of Wycliffe are the emblem of his doctrine, which now is dispersed the world over.”[14]

John Hus: Bohemian Rebel

John Hus (~1369-1415)

Beside John Wycliffe, another light for Christian truth even prior to the Protestant Reformation was John Hus (or Huss). Like Wycliffe, he played an integral role in setting the stage for Reformation.

In the library at Prague, three medallions tell the story of the

14 *Christian History Magazine*, Vol II, No. 2, Issue 3, p. 30.

Protestant Reformation. The first shows Wycliffe, an Englishman, striking sparks from a stone. The second depicts Hus, a Bohemian, kindling a fire from those sparks. And the third portrays Luther, a German holding high the torch. Thus, the medallions serve to artistically narrate the Reformation story from start to finish.

Like Wycliffe, Hus was a Roman Catholic who became increasingly convinced of the papacy's departure from the doctrine of Christ. In his reputable history, Elder Sylvester Hassell comments on the strategic role that Hus played in protesting the abuses of the established church:

> His undoubtedly is the honor of having been the chief intermediary in handing on from Wycliffe to Luther the torch which kindled the reformation, and of having been one of the bravest of the martyrs who have died in the cause of honesty and freedom, of progress and of growth towards the light. He added nothing to the intellectual, but immensely to the moral capital of the world. Seldom have the power of conscience and the imperial strength of a faith rooted in Christ asserted themselves in so commanding and heroic a manner.[15]

Hus was born in Bohemia, the modern Czech Republic, in 1369. The marriage of Anne of Bohemia to Richard II of England established an alliance between the two countries. After Richard's death, Anne returned to Bohemia with the writings of Wycliffe. These writings found their way to the University of Prague where John Hus was a professor. Both in writing and preaching, Hus

15 *Hassell's History*, p. 367.

carried on the tradition of Wycliffe by criticizing clerical abuses and questioning the doctrine of the mass.

Though Hus did not, according to Hassell, discern as much of the truth as did Wycliffe, he yet "taught the Bible doctrine of salvation by the electing love and grace of God, and also the right of private judgment in the interpretation of the Scriptures."[16]

In the year 1407, his right to preach was revoked. Nevertheless, Hus kept on preaching. He insisted that he was prepared to obey the Pope's commands "so far as they agree with the doctrine of Christ, but when I see the contrary, I will not obey them even though you burn my body."[17] Hus was excommunicated, and the city of Prague was placed under an interdict as long as it sheltered "the heretic and his followers."

In 1414, Hus was summoned to appear for trial before the General Council of Constance. He was detained for six months in prison, an experience that he endured humbly. When he was finally brought to trial in 1415, the "kangaroo court" would not permit him to speak in his own defense, even though he was accused of the ridiculous charge of proclaiming himself a fourth person in the Holy Trinity.

The sentence was passed that Hus and his books were to be publicly burned. The bishop shouted, "We commit thy soul to the devil," but Hus replied "And I commit it to the Lord Jesus Christ." A crown reading, "This is an arch heretic," was placed upon his head, and Hus was led to his execution. As they tied him to a pole, he prayed, "Lord Jesus, please have mercy on my enemies." He died singing with a loud voice, "Jesus, Son of the living God, have mercy upon me."

---

16 Ibid.

17 Houghton, *Sketches from Church History,* p. 69.

After the burning of John Hus, an assembly of 54 Bohemian and Moravian nobles endorsed his doctrines and protested the action of the Council of Constance. They formed a league to protect the free preaching of God's word in their country. This "rebellion" was met with a ferocious crusade against Bohemia under Pope Martin V. This bloody war lasted for eleven years with many atrocities, both on the part of the Catholics and the Hussites. But in the end, the Hussites survived. Some of them joined the Reformation of the 16th century, while others maintained a separate identity as the Moravian Brethren.

Just as a "morning star" signals the coming dawn, so the commitment of these nonconformist groups—such as the Waldenses, Lollards and Hussites—to a Bible-centered (as opposed to a tradition-centered) faith and life anticipated a new and brighter day. That long-awaited "dawning" would arrive with the inauguration of the 16th century.

It was in the 1500's that the tide began to turn and the twin strongholds in western Europe of economic and societal feudalism on the one hand, and religious Catholicism on the other would meet with respective dual challenges in the form of the Italian Renaissance and the Protestant Reformation. For the common man, it was indeed a time of hope for liberation from the general ignorance and spiritual darkness that had prevailed during the Medieval Period.

8
The Protestant Reformation
A.D. 1500 - 1600

It has been said that Wycliffe packed a powder keg for Reformation, and Hus wove the fuse. It only remained for someone to ignite the fuse. That someone would prove to be a young German monk named Martin Luther.

Luther never intended to start the Protestant Reformation. By his own admission, he was "utterly clumsy and incapable in the conduct of such high matters...[and] became embroiled in them by accident, not because [he] wanted or intended to do so." Nevertheless, he took the protests of Wycliffe and Hus a step further. "Others before me have contested practice," he said, "I attack doctrine. To contest doctrine is to grab the goose by the neck."

Luther: A Wild Boar Loose in God's Vineyard

Martin Luther was born in 1483 to middle class parents, Hans and Hannah Luther. Hans was a peasant and copper miner who taught that freedom was preferable to power and influence. Martin must have heard his father repeat the motto, "A free peasant is nobody's slave," on more than one occasion.

Though Luther's parents maintained a semblance of religious piety, they were also influenced by various medieval superstitions that were popular in that time. His mother blamed the death of one of her children on a neighbor whom she believed to be a witch. She taught her children that the woods and winds and waters were populated by elves, gnomes, fairies, mermen, mermaids, sprites, and witches.

In 1505 as a student at the University of Erfurt, Luther was caught in a thunderstorm. A bolt of lightning struck him to the ground, and he instinctively cried out to the patron saint of the copper miners, "Saint Anne, help me! I will become a monk."

He kept his vow and entered an Augustinian monastery seeking peace in his soul. He was an extraordinary monk. His biographer states,

> [Luther] fasted sometimes three days on end without a crumb. He laid upon himself vigils and prayers in excess of those stipulated by the rule. He cast off blankets permitted him and well nigh froze himself to death. At times, he was proud of his sanctity and would say, "I have done nothing wrong today." Then misgivings would arise: "Have you fasted enough? Are you poor enough?" He would then strip himself of all save that which decency required.[1]

Luther was such a strict monk because he yearned to compensate for his sins. He said, "I was a good monk, and I kept the rule of my order so strictly that I may say that if ever a monk got to heaven by his monkery, it was I...If I had kept on any longer, I should have killed myself with vigils, prayers, reading, and other work."[2]

---

1 Roland Bainton, *Here I Stand*, p. 34. (Note: Ascetism, or the attempt to achieve righteousness by extreme forms of self-denial and self-punishment, was common in monastic life, but Luther took it to another level.)

2 Ibid.

Martin Luther, Augustinian Monk

Young Martin could never feel, however, that he had satisfied God. He could not find peace. Luther concluded that human beings were incapable of the kind of selflessness that Scripture required. He was haunted by "the righteousness of God." He could not seem to escape the deep awareness of his own guilt and of God's holiness, even though he sometimes spent six hours at a time in the confessional. Once when asked if he did not love God, Luther replied, "Love God? Sometimes, I hate him."

Luther so frequently approached his mentor, Johann von Staupitz, with such extreme doubts and inner turmoil, that Staupitz finally admonished him to "Go out and commit a real sin and then return to the confessional. The murder of one's parents, public vices, blasphemy, adultery, these are sins. You must not inflate your artificial sins out of proportion. If you expect Christ to forgive you, come in with something to forgive instead of all these peccadilloes."[3] On another occasion, Staupitz scolded him. "Man, God is not angry with you. You are angry with God. Don't you know that God commands you to hope?"[4]

In 1510, Luther traveled to Rome in the hope that he would find "salvation." This trip to the "Holy City," however, only filled him with more pain and doubt. He scaled the *Santa Scala* on his knees attempting to free his grandfather Heine Luder from

3 *Christian History Magazine*, Issue 34 (Vol. XI, No. 2), p. 12.

4 Bainton, p. 41.

Purgatory. He said an "Our Father" on each step, but when he reached the top, he was overwhelmed with skepticism. He questioned, "Who knows if it is really true?"

That question echoed with greater frequency over the next few years. His disillusionment with the Established Church's inability to communicate peace and assurance to his soul was growing. He was beginning to question every major doctrine of Catholicism. He was becoming increasingly disenchanted with the idea of salvation by human works.

Martin Luther's growing disillusionment with Catholicism soon came to a head. On October 31, 1517, he posted his famous "95 Theses" to the door of the Castle Church in Wittenberg, Germany. These 95 points of protest boldly exposed the abuse of indulgences[5] A sampling of the 95 Theses is as follows:

Luther Posting the "95 Theses"

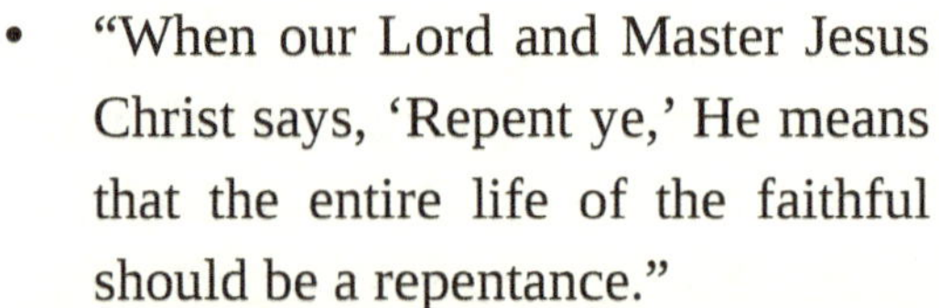

- "When our Lord and Master Jesus Christ says, 'Repent ye,' He means that the entire life of the faithful should be a repentance."
- "This statement cannot be understood of the sacrament of penance, that is of confession and satisfaction, which is administered by the priesthood."
- "They preach human folly who pretend that as soon as money in the coffer rings, a soul from Purgatory springs."

5 The practice of selling "indulgences" consisted of granting clemency or forgiveness for the sins of the deceased in exchange for money.

- "Christians should be taught that whoever sees a person in need and instead of helping him, uses his money for an indulgence, obtains not an indulgence of the Pope, but the displeasure of God."
- "Christians should be taught that the Pope ought and should give his own substance to the poor from whom certain preachers of indulgences extract money, even if he had to sell Saint Peter's Cathedral to do it."
- "Why does not the Pope empty Purgatory for the sake of holy love? For after all, he does release countless souls for the sake of sordid money contributed for the building of a cathedral."

Within two weeks, booksellers utilizing Gutenberg's newly invented printing-press duplicated Luther's *95 Theses* and distributed them, without his permission, across Germany. Within a month, copies had spread throughout Europe.

Johann Tetzel, a Dominican friar, replied with his own "106 Theses," in which he stated, "Christians should be taught that the Pope, by authority of his jurisdiction, is superior to the entire Catholic Church and its Councils, and that they should humbly obey his statutes." Pope Leo X, himself, soon resolved to "quench a monk...Martin Luther by name, and thus smother the fire before it should become a conflagration."

Many of Luther's religious and academic contemporaries refused to debate the theological implications of indulgences. The issue with them was not whether people might draw on the treasury of Christ's merits deposited with the Church in order to alter their standing with God. Instead, they redefined the question in terms of whether or not the church could prescribe doctrine and insist on obedience.

The tension continued to escalate over the subsequent two years as Luther declared that "a simple layman armed with the Scriptures is to be believed above both Pope and Councils without it." In October 1520, the Pope issued a Papal Bull titled *Exsurge Domine* denouncing Luther as a heretic and threatening to excommunicate him if he refused to recant within 60 days.

The Bull began with the words (referring to Psalm 80:13), "*Arise, O Lord, for a wild boar is loose in thy vineyard*." Luther responded by calling the document "the execrable bull of the Antichrist" and publicly burning it, together with the entire canon law at the conclusion of the 60-day grace period.

In the months that followed, Luther published three seminal treatises in which he spelled out the practical consequences of his theology: *An Address to the Christian Nobility*, *The Babylonian Captivity of the Church*, and *On the Freedom of a Christian*. In the first, he argued for the concept that came to be known as "the priesthood of all believers." In the second, he challenged the Roman Catholic idea of seven sacraments and argued for only three: Baptism, the Lord's Supper, and Penance. In the third, he urged that Christians were free from the law (in particular, the man-made laws of the "Established Church"), albeit duty bound to love their neighbors.

Pope Leo's desire to snuff out the flame before it grew into a conflagration would never come to fruition. The only way to reign in this "wild boar" now was to issue an Imperial Edict against him and summon him to appear before Emperor Charles V. The imperial Diet[6] would take place in April 1521.

6 An official Roman assembly in which the Emperor and the empire's semi-sovereign territories and rulers met to adjudicate matters of public concern.

On April 17, 1521, all the forces of "Church" and State converged for an imperial Diet at Worms[7] against Luther. Emperor Charles V personally presided over the Imperial Diet, flanked by 206 persons of rank including dukes, archbishops, and papal nuncios.

The proceedings of the first day ended almost as soon as they began. Luther was asked two questions: 1. Are you the author of the writings displayed on the table? 2. Are you willing to recant the teachings contained in the books which the Church disapproves?

Luther at Worms, April 1521

After examining the pile of books, Luther admitted to being the author. But concerning the second question, Luther requested a time for reflection that he might not act precipitously. The request was granted and the meeting adjourned until the next day.

That night, Luther prayed, "O God, my God, be with me and protect me against my enemies of this world. Thou must do it. Thou alone, for in me is no strength. It is thy cause, O God, not mine. On Thee I rely, not on man, for that would be in vain. Oh God, dost Thou not hear? Do not hide Thy face from me. Thou has called me to this task—I feel it. Be Thou my stay. I ask it in the Name of the Son, Jesus Christ, my protector, my shield, and my defense."

7 A city south of Frankfurt in southwestern Germany.

The next day, Luther was again queried concerning his willingness to recant. He replied, “Unless I am convinced by Sacred Scripture or by evident reason—for Popes and Councils have often erred and contradicted themselves—I cannot recant, for my conscience is captive to the Word of God. To go against conscience is neither right nor safe. Here I take my stand; I can do no other. So help me God. Amen.”

Bedlam erupted in the Diet. Finally, the Emperor rose from his seat and left the proceedings stating that “he could not see how a single monk could be right and the testimony of a thousand years of Christendom be wrong.”

A few days later, Luther left Worms for his home in Wittenberg. Little did he know, however, that the Empire had declared him an outlaw, threatening anyone who gave him food or lodging with “high treason.” As his carriage entered a thick glen, a company of horsemen surrounded Luther's party and kidnapped him. The captors turned out to be allies who were privy to the government’s plot against him. He was stolen away to a remote castle in Wartburg where he was dressed as a knight and addressed by the alias “Squire George.” His room had a retractable stairway to ensure his anonymity. All of this had been arranged for his protection by his close friend and ally, Frederick the Wise.

The Castle at Wartburg

For ten months, Luther was hidden away in Wartburg Castle. He was miserable and did not like living in exile. He improved the opportunity, however, by translating the New Testament into German. Later, he would translate the Old Testament as well.

Martin Luther's new German Bible translated from the *Textus Receptus,*[8] attained instant popularity and set the stage for future translations. William Tyndale would draw heavily from Luther's work in his own translation of the English Bible.

Luther also wrote other treatises while exiled at Wartburg. Perhaps the legend that he once "threw an inkwell at the Devil" in his study at Wartburg Castle is really a metaphorical reference to the way he so effectively used the medium of print as his pulpit during this period in his life.

In 1522, Luther escaped from the castle without Frederick's permission. He returned to Wittenberg and began preaching in his own pulpit. He continued his labors for another twenty years or so and the Reformation movement proceeded apace.

Perhaps his most poignant literary production of these post-Wartburg years was a book written to counter the teaching of Erasmus. It was entitled *The Bondage of the Will.* Erasmus held, with the Roman Catholics, that man's will was not totally depraved by the fall, but was able to contribute something to salvation. Luther insisted that the will of man was bound, not free, and that it could not act beyond the limits of its nature. He also wrote the hymn "A Mighty Fortress Is Our God," which became the battle hymn of the Protestant Reformation.

---

8 The same family of manuscripts later used for the English Authorized Version of 1611.

Ulrich Zwingli, Swiss Reformer

Luther was not the only theologian protesting Catholicism, and Germany was not the only venue of change. The Reformation was simultaneously erupting in other parts of Europe.

In Switzerland, Ulrich Zwingli became increasingly convinced that the key emphases of Catholicism were inconsistent with Holy Scripture. In 1519, he was appointed preacher in the city of Zurich. He accepted the appointment on condition that he would be permitted to preach the pure gospel of Christ. Great crowds attended his ministry.

His followers formed a new religious organization and called it the Reformed Church. It was not long, however, before those committed to Catholicism attempted to suppress Zwingli's influence. They persecuted the Swiss brethren who lived in Catholic cantons. Soon, an army of 8,000 Catholics invaded Zurich. Zwingli himself joined the small counter-force of 2,700 as chaplain. The two sides met in a battle at Cappell in 1531. About 500 Protestants were slain, including Zwingli.

Resorting to the sword to defend themselves against persecution was obviously an unbiblical decision. How different was the reaction of the Anabaptists in Germany who, according to Sylvester Hassell in *History of the Church of God*, "though grievously persecuted by thousands, robbed, imprisoned, tortured, driven with their wives and children from their homes to woods and deserts, yet declared that they would rather die than raise a hand, much less a weapon against their enemies."[9] Nevertheless, so confused were many of the Reformers by Catholicism's marriage of Church and State that they erred in this matter of attempting to advance the kingdom of God by carnal weapons.

9 Hassell, *History of the Church of God*, p. 503.

Though the Reformation in Switzerland was curbed by the Battle of Cappell, it was not completely halted. Zwingli's successors drafted a creed called the "Second Helvetic Confession of Faith," a Confession that is still referenced by Reformed churches today.

John Calvin, French Reformer

At about the same time that Zwingli was active in Switzerland, a French theologian named John Calvin was gaining influence in Paris. In 1535, Calvin moved to Basel, Switzerland where he found refuge and began his attempt to write a systematic theology. The finished product is entitled *Institutes of the Christian Religion.*

A fellow Frenchman named William Farel urged Calvin to relocate to Geneva. Farel and Calvin attempted to remake Geneva into a truly theocratic community. Almost the whole city would come together to hear the Word of God. The education of young people was carefully organized, and family worship was prescribed by ordinance for every citizen.

Geneva became the epicenter of the Reformation, and a haven of refuge to many Protestants whose lives were endangered. Not everyone, however, found a welcome in Geneva. The burning of Michael Servetus for "heresy" on Calvin's watch is a dark blot on the Reformer's legacy, and shows that he, like other Reformers, was not totally free from the errors of his times. He had not escaped the notion that Church and State should mingle.

Calvin is credited with the inception of Presbyterianism. After his death, many of Calvin's emphases were codified at the Synod of Dort (in the Netherlands), recognized today by the TULIP acronym.

Other Reformers could be cited such as John Knox in Scotland and Thomas Cranmer and Hugh Latimer in England. Each had ties to Catholicism, but protested the excesses that had come to characterize Rome.

The reputable Baptist historian William Lumpkin remarks that the Anabaptists had much in common with the Reformers and at first identified with their movements. Yet they eventually distanced themselves from Luther, Zwingli, and Calvin as they discovered remnants of unbiblical notions among the Reformers. One of the primary points of contention was Anabaptist *ecclesiology,* or the doctrine of the church. The reformers vehemently disagreed with the Anabaptist insistence that "the Church is composed only of deliberate followers of Christ, that admission to it is by confession and baptism, that it is autonomous, and that it keeps itself pure by discipline."[10]

Concerning these Anabaptists, we will consider them in Chapter 9. Before we proceed to discuss the particular history of the Baptists, however, it is important to note in greater detail the premier theological controversy of the Reformation.

Calvinism vs Arminianism

The primary conflict among the Protestants during the Reformation was a dispute between John Calvin and Jacob Arminius concerning the doctrine of salvation. It was comparable to the earlier debates between Augustine and Pelagius, and Luther and Erasmus. This controversy would have such lasting consequences that the names of the two men would become a kind of shorthand label for the opposing parties for centuries to come.

10 Wm. Lumpkin, *Baptist Confessions of Faith*, p. 13.

Calvin's emphasis on predestination was gaining wide acceptance within Protestant circles. In the late 1500s, Jacob Arminius, a Dutch theologian at Leiden University, began to challenge Calvin's views. He taught that while God had made salvation possible through Christ, he had left it to the sinner to decide whether or not he would accept it.

Arminius died in 1609. The following year, his followers published articles of "Remonstrance" against Calvin's teaching. They drafted five articles to summarize their beliefs about salvation:

1. On their own, humans can do nothing good.
2. Before the foundation of the world, God chose to save everyone who would freely choose to trust Christ.
3. Jesus died for everyone, but his death only redeems believers.
4. People can choose to reject God's attempts to save them.
5. Scripture is unclear on the question of whether Christians can forfeit their salvation.

So the Arminians espoused partial human depravity, election on the basis of foreseen faith, a general atonement with a special application, resistible grace, and the possibility of a lapse from grace. Acceptance of these "five points of Arminianism" gained momentum over the next few years.

In 1618, a group of Calvin's followers gathered at Dordrecht in The Netherlands to denounce the Arminians. The Synod of Dort drafted five points of their own in answer to the Arminians.

Synod of Dordrecht (1619)

1. Human beings are by nature spiritually dead (Rom. 3:10-12; Eph. 2:1).
2. God's choice of sinners to salvation is unconditional and antecedent to faith in Christ (Jno. 6:44; Rom. 9:10-16).
3. Christ's death atoned only for those who believe in him (Jno. 3:16).
4. When God regenerates a person, that person will neither resist nor reject God's grace (Jno. 6:37, 44).
5. Every regenerate person will persevere in faith until the end Jno. 10:27-28; Rom. 8:29-39).

These "five points of Calvinism" were popularized by the TULIP acronym where the *T* stood for Total depravity, *U* for Unconditional election, *L* for Limited atonement, *I* for Irresistible grace, and *P* for Perseverance of the saints. It is important to note that both camps—the Arminian and the Calvinist—affirm that believing in Jesus Christ, i.e. evangelical faith, accompanies eternal salvation. The Arminian says, “If you are saved, you *must* hear and believe the gospel, and it's up to you whether you do.” The Calvinist says, “If you are saved, you *will* hear and believe the gospel, for God has chosen you to faith.”

Understanding this debate in Christian history, however, helps us to make sense of subsequent developments, both within evangelical Protestantism and among the Baptists. The theological influence of the Reformation inevitably spilled over into Baptist circles in the 17th century and beyond, especially in terms of this controversy between Calvinism and Arminianism. The proliferation of Creeds and Confessions among 17th century Baptists was due in large part to the influence of this debate, and that will be a topic of consideration as we move through Part 5.

9
Reformation & the Baptists in Europe A.D. 1500 - 1600

In large measure, popular historians tend to either entirely overlook or make abbreviated reference to the presence of the Baptists during the Reformation period. But just as pious and independent groups like the Waldenses, Tertullians, Novatians and Lollards maintained a quiet presence since the earliest days of Christian history, Baptist groups continued to practice a simple and unadorned devotion to Christ during this period of tectonic shifts in the Christian landscape. Two particular groups in Europe, the Anabaptists and the Welsh Baptists, will be our focus in this chapter.

The Quiet Faith of the Anabaptists

There is perhaps no more maligned group of Christians than the Anabaptists. Virtually every church historian speaks derogatorily of them. None can dispute, however, that during the Protestant Reformation, Anabaptist groups maintained a quiet existence, separate and apart from Catholics and Protestants alike, as a part of the "free church" tradition.

Anabaptists, meaning "rebaptizers" because they rebaptized people who had been sprinkled as infants, thrived in Germany, The Netherlands, and other parts of Europe. The E*ncyclopedia Britannica* states that the persecutions they endured "were incomparably fiercer than any of the larger Protestant bodies ever underwent."[1] Catholics deemed them rebels because they spurned pedo- (or infant) baptism, refused to acknowledge the authority of Pope and Councils, and insisted on the principle of separation between church and state. Protestants deemed them heretics, traitors, and dangerous radicals. Indeed, some of the doctrinal and political excesses that characterized certain Anabaptists occasioned Protestant disdain, but most Anabaptist adherents were virtuous, pious, and blameless followers of Christ.

Elder Sylvester Hassell states that the Anabaptists "were generally poor, laboring people and their ministers were generally uneducated and labored with their own hands."[2] There was one notable exception to this. The most learned and eloquent minister among the Anabaptists was one Balthasar Hubmaier.

Hubmaier had left Catholicism first, then Protestantism, because he could not find infant baptism taught in the New Testament. He received "believer's baptism" among the Anabaptists and subsequently baptized several hundred others. The reputable historian Philip Schaff says of Hubmaier, "He was perhaps the first who taught the principle of universal religious liberty, on the ground that Christ came not to kill and to burn, but to save, and condemned the employment of force in His kingdom. He was tortured in Switzerland and burned in Vienna (March 10, 1528), going steadfastly to the stake with pious joy. His wife who had encouraged him in his martyr spirit was three days afterward drowned in the Danube."[3]

Perhaps the most celebrated Anabaptist minister of the 16th century was Menno Simons. As a Catholic priest, Simons

1 As quoted in Hassell, *History of the Church of God*, p. 502.
2 Ibid. p. 504.
3 Op Cit.

witnessed the beheading of an Anabaptist and was led on a biblical quest to justify the practice of infant baptism. Conscience compelled him to abandon Catholicism and to unite with the despised Anabaptists in 1536. He traveled extensively throughout Europe, establishing churches, instructing them against revolutionary activities, and insisting on a strict gospel discipline in each congregation. His churches, who called themselves Mennonites, were independent in church government, and some practiced feet washing.

In spite of various heresies charged against the Anabaptists—such as Manichaeism, Arianism, Arminianism, millenarianism, asceticism, universalism, and libertinism—the beliefs of the main body of Anabaptists are expressed in the Swiss Confession of 1527 and the Mennonite Confession of 1580. Those fundamental convictions were as follows:

- Baptism of believers
- Exclusion of unworthy members
- Communion of baptized believers
- Separation from impure churches and the world
- The support of needy pastors by the voluntary offerings of the members
- The condemnation of Christians holding civil office
- Obedience to civil magistrates, except in cases when their commands violated religious conviction
- The disuse of oaths
- A rejection of the use of arms
- A rejection of lawsuits
- A rejection of all forms of violence and worldly amusement
- A rejection of divorce except in cases of adultery.

Elder Hassell comments, "While the true 'Anabaptists' or 'Mennonites' of the sixteenth century had great spiritual light on most other subjects, Bible Baptists of today believe that they were generally in the dark in regard to the conditionality of salvation. The bitter persecutions inflicted upon them, inconsistently and unscripturally, by the Lutherans, Calvinists, and Anglicans who profess to believe the doctrine of predestination, did not incline them to receive that Bible doctrine, nor indeed did they seem to devote any particular attention to its consideration."[4]

The Anabaptists, nevertheless, demonstrate a witness for believer's baptism, congregational independence, and other Baptist distinctives, separate and apart from both Catholicism and Protestantism, during the era of the Reformation. As such, their history provides a valuable insight into a line of Church History beyond the classical context of reference.

Baptists in the Welsh Midlands

When most historians discuss Baptists in Europe in the 16th and 17th centuries, they limit their focus to English Baptists. A more obscure, yet equally viable and arguably more pure Baptist influence, however, existed in Wales at the same time.

Unlike many of the English Baptists, the Welsh Baptists were careful to distinguish themselves from the Protestant Reformation. John Howells, former pastor of Olchon Baptist Church in the Olchon Valley (located on the Wales/England border) wrote, "The genuine Baptist Church needed no reformation, for it never deformed or degenerated itself."[5]

---

4 Hassell, p. 506.

5 As quoted in *Welsh Succession of Primitive Baptist Faith & Practice*, Michael N. Ivey, p. 45.

In his *History of the Welsh Baptists,* Jonathan Davis wrote, "We know that at the Reformation...they had a minister named Howell Vaughn, quite a different sort from Erbury, Wroth, Vavasor Powell, and others who were the great reformers, but had not reformed so far as they ought to have done, in the opinion of the Olchon Baptists...We know that the reformers were for mixed communion, but the Olchon Baptists received no such practices. In short, these were plain, strict Apostolic Baptists. They would have order and no confusion, the word of God their only rule."[6]

Most historians who mention the Welsh Baptists cite the fact that their churches were situated in the mountainous regions, and thus were relatively inaccessible to pervasive traffic from outsiders, as the reason they were largely unaffected by the doctrine and practices of the Reformers. J. R. Graves wrote in *Orchard's History,* "Welsh Baptists contend that principles of the gospel were maintained pure and unalloyed in the recesses of their mountainous principality all through the dark reign of popery."[7] And Cathcart wrote in his history, "It is commonly believed that all through the dark reign of popery, in the seclusions of her valleys and the fastnesses of her mountains, there were those who preserved the ancient purity of doctrine and worship."[8]

Why is it important to document the existence of Baptists in the Welsh Midlands who were largely unaffiliated with the English Baptists of the 17th century? It is important because many of the English Baptists, as we will note in Part 5, tended toward

6 Ibid. p. 45.
7 Ivey, p. 46.
8 Ibid.

ecumenism.[9] The political situation in England made it necessary for English Baptists to align themselves with Presbyterianism, as the English Baptist ministers who signed the London Confession of Faith in 1687 admitted in the "Preface" to that document:

> "...and finding no defect in this regard, in that fixed on by the Assembly [the Westminster Assembly], and after them by those of the congregational way [the Savoy Declaration of Faith], we did readily conclude it best to retain the same order in our present Confession, hereby declaring before God, angels, and men, our hearty agreement with them in that wholesome Protestant doctrine, which with so clear evidence of Scriptures, they have asserted."[10]

The result was a document that was almost a verbatim copy of the Westminster Confession of Presbyterians, as we will further discuss in Part 5.

Olchon Church is generally considered the "mother church" of the Welsh Baptists. Documentation exists connecting the churches of the Welsh Midlands, including Hereford, Tewksbury, Moreton, Burton, and Leonminster with Olchon Church, so that it may be safely assumed that these churches were in general doctrinal agreement.

What did the Welsh Baptists believe? Besides a common conviction for the practice of believers' baptism and closed communion, they espoused a clear doctrine of salvation by grace alone, apart from human agency. Owen writes concerning the Midland brethren, stating that they "could find no scope in [their]

9 *Ecumenism* is the pursuit of unity in spite of historical divisions (due to doctrinal and practical differences) among various Christian groups.

10 Preface to "The London Confession of Faith," 1687.

rigorous creed for the operation of any human agency in winning the unconverted to the gospel of Jesus Christ. God saves all who are predestinated, and no man can help or hinder His sovereign and effectual grace."[11]

In 1655, the seven churches comprising the Midland Association in Wales composed a Confession of Faith, from which the key points of emphasis of Welsh Baptist theology may be deduced. Those points are as follows:

- The doctrine of the Trinity
- The inspiration and sufficiency of Scripture
- The doctrine of inherent depravity
- The doctrine of sovereign and unconditional election
- The incarnation of Christ for the purpose of redeeming the elect
- The inability of men apart from regenerating grace to believe
- Justification by Christ alone, apprehended [that is, understood or subjectively grasped] by faith
- The bodily resurrection and heavenly session of Christ
- The final resurrection of the dead.

A careful examination of the Midland Confession of 1655 reveals an amazing similarity to modern day Primitive Baptist theology.

The contemporaneous presence of these established Baptist groups during the period in which Protestantism was born in western Europe, together with their resolve to remain separate, resisting the pull of ecumenical peer-pressure to adopt the Protestant cause, is a testament to how the Baptists of the 16th and

11 Ivey. p. 70.

17th centuries maintained a sense of historical connection to their post-apostolic ancestors within the "free-church" tradition.

PART 5

The Age of Religious Liberty

A.D. 1600 - 1900

10
The English Baptists
A.D. 1600 – 1700

The 17th century A.D. is pivotal in Baptist history. Suddenly in this century, Baptists in Europe broke with historical precedent and began to issue confessional statements like the Lutherans, Presbyterians, and Congregationalists.

In his book, *Baptist Confessions of Faith*, W. L. Lumpkin cites at least ten Baptist Confessions published in the sixteen hundreds. It is not inappropriate to question the reasons for this proliferation of Baptist Confessions in the 1600s, especially in lieu of the Baptist's historical rejection of Creeds and Confessions. It is also not inappropriate to question why certain Baptist ministers that lived in this century—men like John Gill, William Kiffin, John Bunyan, Samuel Richardson, and Hansard Knollys—have been held in such high esteem by Baptists in subsequent generations.

I must admit that I have no particular personal fascination with or allegiance to the 17th century Baptists, apart from a general respect for servants of Christ who are faithful to their Lord, and the role these men played in Baptist history. Though I have no doubt that many of these men were pious and devoted servants of the Lord Jesus Christ, I do not think it either prudent or accurate to look to any man, or group of men, as standards of orthodoxy.

Perhaps the "larger than life" reputation some of these men now enjoy is due to the sheer volume of literature they left as a legacy to us. Because Baptists maintained an obscure and persecuted existence throughout the Dark Ages and the first one-hundred years of the Protestant Reformation, little to no record from the pens of Baptist leaders exists. The sudden emergence of reams of literature from the 17thcentury, consequently—whether we think of Gill's expositions, Bunyan's allegories, or the theological explanations offered in the Confessions—provides modern Baptists with the most ancient literary resource of Baptist thought available and a touchstone to Baptist heritage. I suspect that the sheer antiquity of this proliferation of Baptistic material in the 17th century has the potential to establish it as an authoritative source in the minds of many sincere believers.

Whatever the reasons may be for much of the contemporary fascination with this period, I acknowledge that for the first time in recorded Church History, Baptists emerged in the 17th century with a distinctive and traceable identity, separate from other Christian groups.

Baptist influence in England likely began in 1616 with Henry Jacob's exile from Holland. Jacob gathered a church of like-minded people together on the basis of a profession of individual faith and a mutual covenant. Some of Jacob's people were Puritans who were loyal to (though seeking to reform) the Church of England, and others were Separatists who rejected all connection with the Established Church.

In the 1630s, Jacob's church divided over the question of the validity of baptism administered by a parish (i.e. Anglican) clergyman, as well as the question of infant baptism. In 1638, the church amicably dismissed another group whose members held that baptism should only be administered to regenerated believers. The "dismissed" group was led by John Spilsbury and is considered to be the first Particular Baptist Church in England. Soon, Spilsbury and his church realized that "baptism ought to be by dipping the body into the water, resembling burial and rising again."[1]

Spilsbury's group was called "Particular" because they believed that the redemption wrought out by Christ was particular and definite in its scope. This label served to distinguish them from the General Baptists who believed that the extent of the atonement was indiscriminate and general. The General Baptists tended to be more Arminian in doctrine, teaching that Christ died for all. The Particulars emphasized the doctrines of election and predestination, teaching that Christ died for the elect and actually secured eternal salvation for them.

Growing Persecution Against the Baptists

An understanding of the political climate of 17th century England is crucial to the explanation of Baptist migration to America during this century and the next. It also explains why there was a sudden explosion of Baptist creedal statements in the 17th century, a phenomenon (again) unknown among the Baptists prior to this time.

The Anglican Church was the established Church in England, but the remarkable growth the Baptists were experiencing had necessarily attracted the attention of the Established Church. With the heightened awareness of the Baptist's growing popularity with the public, there was a corresponding and increasing anti-Baptist sentiment within Anglicanism, particularly for the Particular Baptists. Religious liberty, a distinctively Baptist principle, was increasingly framed as a tenet that promoted and encouraged civil disobedience. Soon, a public relations campaign targeting the reputation of the Baptists took shape. Various slanderous

1 W. L. Lumpkin, *Baptist Confessions of Faith*, p. 143.

accusations such as insubordination, treason, and cannibalism were hurled at the Baptists in the public square.

In his book entitled *Welsh Succession of Primitive Baptist Faith and Practice*, Michael Ivey writes, "In a desire to reveal the orthodoxy of their faith and practice, and also to demonstrate their separate identity from the General Baptists...the Particular Baptists met in London in 1644 and composed their Confession of Faith."[2] Elder Sylvester Hassell concurs that the first London Confession was composed with a view to answering critics, dispelling myths, and showing the Baptist's solidarity with accepted Protestant traditions: "In 1644," Hassell writes, "they numbered seven churches in London and forty-seven in the country; and the same year, three years before the Westminster Confession, in answer to the calumnies of Daniel Featley, an Episcopalian clergyman, the seven London churches published, in fifty-two articles, a Confession of Faith, showing that, in all important doctrinal principles, the Baptists agreed with the orthodox Reformed Churches."[3]

This quasi-ecumenical design to show solidarity with the Presbyterians was successful. In 1647, the London Confession was recognized by the English Parliament, and the Particular Baptists were granted official toleration. They could meet and worship without reprisal or recrimination.

Official toleration was short lived, however. With the rise of Charles II in 1660, religious liberty was effectively revoked. Over the next 25 years, Dissenters to the Established Church were systematically and increasingly persecuted. Even with the

2 Michael Ivey, *Welsh Succession of Primitive Baptist Faith & Practice*, p. 30.

3 C.B. & Sylvester Hassell, *History of the Church of God*, p. 524.

installation of Oliver Cromwell and Presbyterians to positions of leadership within the English commonwealth, a reluctance to tolerate dissent and a desire to promote religious conformity prevailed. James Tull writes, "The Presbyterians intended for the church to be a national church, embracing the whole population in its membership. Dissent was not to be allowed; membership was compulsory. Everyone was to have his children baptized and to pay tithes. On this point, there was little difference from the church as already established."[4]

In 1662, for instance, the Act of Uniformity required the use of the Anglican *Book of Common Prayer* in all religious meetings. The penalty for rebellion was heavy fines and imprisonment. The Conventicle Act was reinstituted in 1664, forbidding non-conformist religious gatherings of more than four people over the age of 16. In 1665, the Five Mile Act prohibited non-conformist ministers from preaching within five miles of any city that had an Established Church within its boundaries. It further prevented any non-Anglican from teaching in a public or private school.

In 1670, another Conventicle Act was passed allowing the Crown to seize all property of repeat offenders. Those who acted as informants were provided one-third of all property seized, so this law tended to promote a culture of corruption. The Test Act of 1673 barred non-conformists, i.e. Baptists, from holding civil or military office, and The Clarendon Code permitted public beatings and even capital execution of dissenters.

It was during this era of religious persecution that a window of opportunity briefly opened. In 1689, William and Mary ascended to the throne and a new Act of Toleration was passed. This Act did not grant total religious freedom, but it did permit non-

---

4 James Tull, *Shapers of Baptist Thought*, p. 11.

conformists to worship without penalty. It was during this brief window of liberty that the Baptists in London decided to ratify a new Confession of Faith that might be acceptable to the Crown. Representatives of 100 Baptist congregations met in London, revised a couple sections of the accepted Westminster Confession of Faith, and adopted it as a statement of their faith.

That the 1689 London Confession was an ecumenical document is clearly stated by those who drafted it. In the Preamble, these Baptist leaders expressed their "...hearty agreement with them [i.e. Presbyterians and Congregationalists] in that wholesome protestant doctrine, which with so clear evidence of the Scriptures they have asserted...and finding no defect in this regard in that fixed on by the Assembly, and after them by those of the Congregational way, we did readily conclude best to retain the same order in our present Confession."

Such an attempt to gain acceptance, however, was not as successful as they had hoped. The Baptists continued to suffer persecution at a level of intensity even greater than the Congregationalists or any other group. This persecution would eventually drive them to seek asylum from political oppression in the New World.

11
The Baptists in America
A.D. 1600 - 1900

Religious persecution arising from political tensions in Europe compelled numerous Baptists to flee to America. In 1638, Dr. John Clark (a physician) and eleven other persons formed the first Baptist Church in America at Newport, Rhode Island.[1] Unlike Roger Williams (who is often credited with the founding of the first Baptist Church), Clark was not in the midst of a "theological journey," but was a strong proponent of the Covenant of Grace. In his book *Welsh Succession of Primitive Baptist Faith and Practice,* Elder Mike Ivey presents a convincing case that Newport Church was "primitive Baptist" in its faith and practice.[2] Clark claimed "that there is no preparation necessary to obtain Christ...nothing can be done by man; there is nothing that he can do to bring down salvation from heaven to earth. For what has to be done has already been done and done by God, not by man."[3]

Elder Obadiah Holmes succeeded Clark as pastor of Newport Church in 1651. Holmes was also committed to proclaiming the doctrines of sovereign grace. The following are a few of his doctrinal sentiments taken from the *Last Will and Testament of Obadiah Holmes:*

1 Elder Lee Hanks, *The Church of God*, p. 102.

2 Ivey, p. 79.

3 Dr. John Clark, *Ill News from New England: Or a narrative of New England Persecution*, p. 42.

- Concerning election: “I believe that God has laid the iniquity of all His elect and called ones upon Him [Christ].”
- Concerning eternal security: “I believe that all those that are in His covenant of grace shall never fall away or perish, but shall have life in the Prince of life, the Lord Jesus Christ.”
- Concerning regeneration: “I believe that no man can come to the Son, but they that are drawn by the Father to Him, and they that come, He will in no wise cast away. I believe none has power to choose salvation or to believe in Christ, for life is the gift only of God.”

Holmes taught that the gospel “begets souls to the truth” and “feeds the church,” but avoids any intimation that the gospel is instrumental in the new birth. His statements demonstrate “a clear understanding of both eternal salvation and gospel deliverance.”[4]

Some things in the New World were really no different for Baptists than they had been in the Old World. Both Elder Clark and Elder Holmes suffered terrible persecutions from those loyal to the Church of England, as well as Puritan detractors in the Colonies. In 1651, the two preachers were arrested and charged with holding an unlawful worship service as they visited in the Massachusetts home of a shut-in member of Newport Church named Brother Witter.[5] Both ministers were held in prison awaiting either the payment of a steep fine or a public flogging. After approximately three weeks, Elder Clark was released,[6] but Elder Holmes remained incarcerated.

As time passed, it became evident that Elder Holmes did not intend to pay his £30 fine. On September 5, he was publicly

4 Ivey, p. 88.

5 Ibid. pp. 80-81.

6 Some conjecture that an anonymous person paid his fine of £20.

flogged at the whipping post near the Old State House in Boston. Michael Ivey writes, "Elder Holmes was beaten with thirty lashes. The Executioner spat upon his hands, and with a scourge of three leather straps, he beat Elder Holmes until his back was laid open to the bone, his flesh raw and bleeding. The beating complete, Elder Holmes was untied from the whipping post and led back to his cell. As he was led away he turned to his executioner and said, 'Sir, you have struck me as with roses'."[7]

Welsh Tract Church

In 1701, Welsh Tract Church was constituted in Newark, Delaware. It has the distinction of being the first official "Primitive" or "Old School" Baptist Church in America. It was one of five constituent churches that eventually formed the Philadelphia Association in 1707. That Welsh Tract Church was "primitive" in its theology is clearly evinced in its 1716 Principles of Faith in which the members affirm their conviction for believer's baptism, the doctrine of election, and the final perseverance[8] of the saints.[9]

Elder Lee Hanks stated in the early 1900s, "Old Welsh Tract Church, which was constituted...more than two hundred years ago is still in existence, coming down to us from Wales without change...This Welsh Tract Church is a Hardshell Church."[10]

---

7 Ivey. p. 83.

8 Like others in that generation, the Welsh Tract brethren incorrectly used this term as a synonym for "final preservation."

9 *The History of Welsh Tract Church and the Life of Elder John Green Eubanks*, p. 4.

10 Hanks, *The Church of God*, p. 109.

Hopewell Church

On April 23, 1715, Hopewell Church was constituted with twelve members in Hopewell, New Jersey. It was organized on the following eight fundamental principles:

1. The three-oneness of God.
2. His self-existence and sovereignty.
3. The total depravity of the natural man.
4. The eternal, personal, unconditional election of all the members of the body of Christ.
5. The specialty and definiteness of the atonement.
6. The necessity of a spiritual birth in order to worship God in spirit and in truth.
7. The sovereign and efficacious operation of Divine Grace upon all the vessels of mercy.
8. The baptism of believers by immersion.

Historian J. H. Grimes states that "This church has never varied from these principles for over two hundred years. Few churches have done more in the formation of our denominational life in America."[11] Elder Lee Hanks makes the following editorial comment concerning Welsh Tract and Hopewell Churches: "Those two churches referred to above were organized true old Baptist Churches about 100 years before modern missions entered America. They, and many more old Baptist Churches in America, are older than the Mission Baptists."[12]

11 As quoted in Hanks, p. 110.
12 Ibid. p. 110.

The Regular and Separate Baptists

To make sense of Baptist history in America, it is important to understand the difference between the Separates and the Regulars. The Regular Baptists had a strong presence on the eastern seaboard, primarily in Coastal North Carolina, the Tidewater region of Virginia, and further north. They were strongly creedal and emphasized the importance of a ministry trained with a classical education. The Philadelphia and Kehukee Associations were dominated by the Regulars.

The Separate Baptists thrived primarily in the South under the ministry of Elders Shubal Stearns and Daniel Marshall. Elder Sylvester Hassell, an ordained minister in the Kehukee Association, writes of them, “These Separates first arose in New England and made their way eventually into the states of Virginia, North Carolina, South Carolina, and Georgia.”[13] The Sandy Creek Association of North Carolina, and the Virginia Separate Baptist Association (which eventually gave rise to the Albemarle, Middle District, Roanoke, and Mountain Associations, as well as others) were affiliated with the Separates. The Separate Baptists spread westward into Kentucky (under the ministry of Squire Boone in 1779) and Mississippi.

In 1742, the Regular Baptists of the Philadelphia Association adopted the 1689 London Confession of Faith and renamed it “The Philadelphia Confession” The Separates, however, were very skeptical of Confessional statements. When the Ketocton Association (affiliated with the Regulars) sent messengers to the Sandy Creek Association in both 1763 and 1769, the Separates graciously resisted[14] the overture because the Ketocton was identified with the Philadelphia Confession of Faith. Robert

13 Hassell, *History of the Church of God*, p. 697.

Semple notes, "A more serious and real objection was that the Philadelphia Confession, some parts of which they considered objectionable, might come to bind them too much." Elder Mike Ivey comments, "The Separates rejected the authority of uninspired creeds and believed the Regulars placed too much emphasis upon the London Confession, allowing it to assume the same weight of authority as inspired scripture."[15]

In 1777, however, four Separate Baptist Churches and six Regular Baptist Churches united in the reformed Kehukee Association, and in 1784, the newly-constituted Georgia Association included both Separate and Regular Baptists. Neither the newly-constituted Georgia nor the reformed Kehukee Association, however, adopted the Philadelphia Confession of Faith, but drafted their own Statements of Faith that closely resemble a typical Primitive Baptist Church's Articles of Faith today, both in content and style.

For the most part, the Regulars were more formal and theologically-inclined, while the Separates were more simple and experientially-inclined. No doubt, there were some among the Regulars who valued a simple and heartfelt religion and some among the Separates who shared the Regular's insistence on precise theology. The primary distinction between the two groups, however, centered on this subject of Creeds and Confessions.

John Sparks, a United Baptist minister in Eastern Kentucky, traces virtually every modern day brand of Baptist in Appalachia

---

14 They wrote: "Excuse us in love; for we are acquainted with our own order, but not so well with yours; and if there is a difference, we might jump into that which will make us rue it." (from Benedict's *History of the Baptist Denomination in America*, pp 51-52).

15 Ivey, *Welsh Succession,* p. 102 (footnote 2)

to Elder Shubal Stearns and the Separate Baptists.[16] He is probably correct that Primitives, Free Wills, Uniteds, Old Regulars, Landmarks and Independent Missionarys within Appalachia each have some kind of tie, at least culturally speaking, to the Separate Baptists. It is also true, however, that a number of Baptist denominations outside of the Appalachian subculture were influenced by the various convictions and emphases of the Regular Baptists.

In my opinion, modern day Primitive Baptists seem to be a blend of the substantive theology of the Regulars (though maintaining the Separate's suspicion of creedalism) and the heartfelt experience of the Separates (while maintaining the Regular's suspicion of emotionalism). I think Primitives today have the best of both worlds.

The effort to unify the Regulars and the Separates, however, would be short-lived. Fullerism had invaded Baptist ranks in England and would soon spread to the Baptists in America. By 1792, doctrinal fissures of no small significance would begin to form in the landscape of American Baptists, opening a chasm of theological difference in 1832 that would be irreparable.

The Baptist Division of 1832

These doctrinal fissures that divided the Baptists between Old School and New School in 1832 were due in large measure to the influx of "Fullerism" into Baptist culture in America. Andrew Fuller, founder of the Baptist Missionary Society in Kettering, England in 1792, is credited with giving Baptists a theology of

---

16 John Sparks, *The Roots of Appalachian Christianity: The Life and Legacy of Elder Shubal Stearns,* University of Kentucky Press, 2003.

missions. His ideas spread like wildfire, not only among the English Baptists but also, in America.

The story is that the English Baptists objected to the idea of evangelizing the lost or offering salvation to sinners. So, Fuller wrote T*he Gospel Worthy of All Acceptation*, in which he attempted to affirm his belief in the doctrines of grace while insisting on the free offer of the gospel to all. This necessarily meant that he must attempt to harmonize divine sovereignty and human responsibility. He wrote,

> "The truth is there are but two ways for us to take. One is to reject them both, [i.e. Divine sovereignty and human responsibility] and the Bible with them, on account of its inconsistencies; the other is to embrace them both, concluding that as they are both revealed in Scripture, they are both true and both consistent, and that is owing to the darkness of our understanding that they do not appear so to us."

Two contemporaries among the English Particulars published challenges to Fuller's views. William Rushton wrote *A Defense of Particular Redemption*, and Joseph Hussey wrote *God's Operations of Grace, but No Offers of Grace.* Neither book, however, succeeded in stemming the tide of Fullerism.

William Carey leaned heavily on Fuller as the theologian who could clearly enunciate a doctrine of missions. Carey would go to India, he said, "like a man let down into a well by a bucket, while Fuller and others held the rope on the other end."

Timothy George of Southern Seminary in Louisville, Kentucky writes, "Andrew Fuller's work made perhaps the most notable contribution towards providing a missionary theology and incentive for world evangelism in the midst of a people both Calvinistic and church oriented. He helped to link the earlier Baptists, whose chief concern was the establishment of ideal New Testament congregations, with those in the nineteenth century driven to make the gospel known worldwide. His contribution helped to guarantee that many of the leading Baptists of the 1800s would typify evangelism and world missions. Charles Spurgeon and J.P. Boyce would be fervent evangelical Calvinists."[17]

Perhaps the best analysis of Fuller's theology comes from the late Elder Sylvester Hassell. Hassell remarks,

> In his writings, Mr. Fuller admits that the Scriptures clearly ascribe both repentance and faith to divine influence; and he professes himself to be a strict Calvinist or predestinarian, notwithstanding this admission and profession, and his attributing, both in conversion and in death, all his salvation to the mere, free, sovereign, efficacious grace of God, he maintains that the prophets, and Christ, and his apostles gave *the most unlimited invitations to unconverted hearers* of the gospel, and so should all gospel ministers do; that the obligations of men to repentance and faith are universal; that man's inability is not proper or physical, but only figurative or moral; that man is able to comply with all that God requires at his hand; that all his misery arises from his *voluntary* abuse of mercy and his *willful* rebellion against God; that it is not a want of ability, but of inclination, that proves his ruin; that men have the same *power,* strictly speaking, before they are wrought upon by the Holy Spirit as after, and before conversion as after; that the work of the Spirit endows us with no new rational powers, nor any powers that are necessary to moral agency. He allows

17 Timothy George, *Theologians of the Baptist Tradition,* 2001.

that "these principles may be inconsistent with the doctrines of grace," but he maintains that "both are scriptural and therefore true"—that "we must receive both the general precepts and invitations of scripture and the declarations of salvation as being a fruit of electing love." Though in one article admitting that the evidence of our interest in the blessings of eternal life must be internal, yet he, in another article, says that "the terms hunger, thirst, labor, heavy laden, etc. do not denote spiritual desires and do not mark out the persons who are entitled to come to Christ." In accordance with this Fullerite principle, I myself heard the most learned Fullerite in North Carolina declare in preaching upon Isaiah lv.1 (55:1) that the address of the prophet applied to *every human being for that all men thirst after something*. While at times apparently delighting to stigmatize "Hyper-Calvinism" as "Antinomianism," and inconsistent with genuine conversion, Mr. Fuller admits that some adherents of this system may have true religion; and, in another article, he declares that *all men by nature are real Antinomians*, for Paul says that the carnal (or unrenewed) mind is enmity against God, not subject to His law, neither indeed can be. William Huntington, S.S. (sinner saved), is regarded by many genuine Baptists in England and America as one of the most spiritual writers of the present century; but Mr. F says that he never saw any marks of genuine religion in Huntington's writings. I'm glad to see that in one place, Mr. Fuller, the standard of the New School Baptists in England and The United States, declares that he "*never imagined himself infallible.*" In this candid statement, all Bible Baptists will heartily agree with him, especially after having read the perfectly fair exhibition of his inconsistencies just given. The *Bible*, however, such Baptists do believe to be *infallible* and therefore not to contain any pair of Mr. Fuller's inconsistencies, as truth cannot be inconsistent with itself. Many of Mr. Fuller's expressions in regard to the ability and power of the unrenewed mind go far beyond the Arminianism of James Arminius, John Wesley, and Richard Watson, who declare that the unrenewed will and all the other faculties of the unrenewed mind are dead in trespasses and sins. Paul declares that "the carnal mind cannot be subject to the law of God;" that "the natural man cannot know the things of the Spirit of God;" and Christ declares that "the world cannot receive the Spirit of truth;" and that "no man can come unto Him except the Father draw him." What then shall we think of Mr. Fuller's fine-spun metaphysics about unrenewed human ability? How can any believer in the Scriptures believe a word of it? It is the superficial declaration of the Roman Catholic Council of Trent that Divine commands necessarily imply human ability—*just as though man had never fallen.* Though man has fallen and become unable to obey the commandments of God, the nature and law and requirements of God are unchanged and unchangeable. The gospel addresses of the Scriptures are addressed, we believe, to gospel characters—to those persons who have *spiritual life, hearing, needs, and appetites.* These limitations are either directly expressed or implied by the circumstances. Even the letter of the word, where there is any fullness of narration, and the dictates of common sense teach this important fact. Inspired men could, far better than we, read the hearts of those whom they addressed, and they addressed hearers of different characters and therefore used sometimes the imperative and sometimes the indicative mood. God's under-shepherds are directed, *not to create* but, to *tend* to the flock. I cannot conceive what benefit can be supposed by a believer in sovereign and efficacious grace to be derived from universally and untruthfully extending the comforting spiritual addresses of the gospel to those declared in

> the Scriptures to be dead in trespasses and sins—Christ expressly forbids that pearls should be cast before swine, Matt. vii.6 [7:6]. Unless the Spirit of God first come and impart Divine life and light to the hearer, such addresses will be forever and totally vain. The imperative mood has no more power than the indicative mood, in the mouth of a preacher, to awaken the dead to life. No language or labor of man, and no fact in creation or providence, independently of the Divine Spirit, has the slightest efficacy to take away the sinner's heart of stone and give him a heart of flesh. I do not deny that the minister may at times have a Divine persuasion that some of his hearers are spiritually alive, and that he may not then properly address them in the imperative mood.[18]

The primary emphasis of Fuller that brought objection from Primitive Baptists in America was his insistence on "duty-faith." He taught that every person was duty-bound to exercise saving faith in Jesus Christ. He also taught that human beings have an inherent rational-moral ability to hear, understand, and believe the gospel, thus an inherent ability to exercise faith.

Because of Fuller's growing influence on the American Baptists, both the question of "missions" and the instrumentality of the gospel in evangelizing the lost grew into a theological chasm. By 1832, the Old School Baptists determined that it was necessary to distance themselves from the innovations of the modern missionary movement.

They met at Black Rock Church in Maryland and issued an "address" detailing various points of their objection to the doctrinal and practical aberrations of Fullerism. Thus was born

18 C. B. & Sylvester Hassell, *History of the Church of God*, pp. 338-340.

the division between Old School (or Primitive) Baptists and the New School (or Missionary) Baptists.

The Baltimore Association in Maryland issued the Black Rock address in 1832 outlining the reasons as stated by Primitive Baptists for the separation from the New School Baptists. That document, together with the Kehukee Declaration, objects primarily to practical innovations (i.e. Sunday Schools, Mission Boards, Instrumental Music in public worship, Bible Societies, and the proliferation of parachurch organizations) that had spawned among a number of churches to accommodate the theology of Andrew Fuller. This separation resolved the doctrinal and practical tensions for the next half-century or so. Near the end of the 19th century, however, a few ministers arose among the Primitive Baptists who attempted to resurrect Fullerite, i.e. gospel agency in regeneration, ideas. Some others began to promote Parkerism, i.e. the absolute predestination of all things, to the confusion of the Old School churches.

The time period surrounding 1900, therefore, was a very trying time for the Primitive Baptists in America. Several noteworthy literary publications from that period served as a standard lifted against these doctrinal challenges.

Thoughts on the Will (1899)

Elder J. H. Oliphant from Crawfordsville, Indiana published *Thoughts on the Will* in 1899 to counter the growing threat of "absolutism." Elder Oliphant's correspondence with Elder Silas Durand (an "absoluter) was also published near this time.

"Absolutism," or *determinism*, asserts that God's decree of predestination applies not only to things eternal, i.e. the eternal salvation of God's elect, but also to things temporal, i.e. the events and circumstances of daily life. This "absolute predestinarian" view tends to deny the voluntary and conditional nature of discipleship, insisting that "God has from eternity ordained whatsoever comes to pass." It teaches that everything that happens in time and eternity is God's will, else it never would have happened.

Elder Oliphant responded to this growing threat of "passive obedience" by affirming that the will of man is actively involved in matters of discipleship, though not in matters of eternal salvation. In fourteen powerfully reasoned chapters, he insisted that sentient creatures are under the moral government of God and that this "voluntariness" distinguishes humans from inanimate objects that are controlled by the sheer force of physical law. Oliphant's clear distinction between the exclusive nature of God's will in eternal salvation and the inclusive nature of man's will in biblical discipleship challenged both the Fullerite and the Parkerite emphases.

The Fulton Footnotes (1900)

The very next year, fifty-one Primitive Baptist ministers (including Oliphant, S. F. and Claude H. Casey, and Lee Hanks) met at Fulton, Kentucky to attempt to stem the tide of this growing doctrinal crisis threatening the peace of the churches. They aimed to draft a document that would establish a benchmark for doctrinal harmony among the churches. They decided to use the 1742 Philadelphia Confession of Faith and to add editorial comments to unclear sections of that Confession by means of various "footnotes."

The resulting *Fulton Confession of Primitive Baptists* did not produce its intended effect of unifying the churches. In just a few short years, both the "absolute predestinarian" and the "progressive" groups split from the Old Line. This effort did produce, however, greater theological precision concerning the issues in dispute.

Two particular passages from the Fulton document are noteworthy. First, the brethren who met at Fulton, Kentucky were very careful to emphasize *a distinction between unconditional eternal salvation and conditional gospel salvation*, a distinction both the Fullerite and the Absolute Predestinarian groups denied.

In commenting on Chapter XVI, Section 3 of this Primitive Baptist Confession, the Fulton brethren wrote,

> We believe the Scriptures teach that there is a time salvation received by the heirs of God distinct from eternal salvation, which does depend upon their obedience. The people of God receive their rewards for obedience in this life only. We believe that the ability of the Christian is the unconditional gift of God.[19]

They further commented, "The act of God necessary to our regeneration must, in some sense, be distinguished from his act necessary to our obedience. We are never commanded to be born again, but in hundreds of places, we are called on to obey. We are passive in regeneration, but in obedience, we are active...There could be no such thing as obedience or disobedience independent of the will. Men do not neglect to be born again, but they do neglect their duty."[20]

---

19 *The Primitive Baptist Confession of Faith of 1900, Fulton, Kentucky,* "Appendix," p. 101.

20 Ibid. p. 102.

Secondly, in response to the Confessional statement "God hath decreed...from all eternity...all things whatsoever come to pass…", the Fulton brethren *distinguished between God's attitude toward sin and His attitude toward holiness.* They wrote,

> We insist that we should not use language implying that God's attitude to sin is the same as his attitude to holiness, for this tends to destroy the distinction between right and wrong.[21]

More historical events in the 1900s that demonstrate this tension between Fullerism and the Old School Baptists could be cited. *The Trial & Decision of Mount Carmel Church*, a 1909 account published by Elder R. H. Pittman, documented how this larger "denominational" crisis was played out in a struggle between two groups for control of the property of Mount Carmel Church in Luray, VA. That crisis was simply another example of the extent to which the theological innovations of Andrew Fuller and his subscribers within Primitive Baptist ranks fostered division among the churches.

In time, the tensions between the Primitive and the Mission Baptists somewhat relaxed, as each went its own way and sought to be true to its respective ideology. Periodically, however, public debates would be held between the two groups in an attempt to win momentum with the public. Elders Oliphant, C. H. Cayce, and others represented the Old School Baptists in a number of these debates. Perhaps the seminal debate was an 1887 discussion between Elder Lemuel Potter, who represented the "Regular Old School Baptists," and Elder W. P. Throgmorton, who represented the "Missionary Baptists." It was held in Fulton, Kentucky on the

21 Op Cit., p. 100.

question, "Who are the Primitive Baptists?" Of course, Potter argued that the doctrine and practice of the "Old School" was consistent with the primitive pattern, and Throgmorton insisted that the "New School" folks were the original Baptists. Each side claimed victory, but suffice it to say that neither group succeeded in convincing the other of its position.

A Chronicle of 19th Century Baptist History

A helpful book detailing the tensions between the Old and New School Baptists, entitled *Fifty Years Among the Baptists*, was written in 1860 by David Benedict, a New School minister and historian, in which the author chronicled five decades of developments among the American Baptists from 1800 to 1850.

In Section 1 (the decade 1800 through 1810), Benedict speaks about leading ministers like John Gano,[22] Jesse Mercer[23] and others. At this point, Baptist churches were experiencing steady growth, albeit suffering reprisals and prejudices in numerous places.

The second decade (1811-1820) was characterized by what Benedict describes as a pivotal event in American Baptist history, namely the conversion to the Baptist camp of two

22 Gano, a Regular (or Particular) Baptist minister, served as Chaplain for George Washington's regiment during the Revolutionary War. In 1759, he was appointed by the Philadelphia Association to visit Sandy Creek Association (NC) where Elder Shubal Stearns and the Separate Baptists held their 2nd Associational Session.

23 A young minister in the early 1800s, Jesse Mercer rose in prominence among the Georgia Baptists, along with Abraham Marshall (firstborn son of Elder Daniel Marshall and Martha Stearns Marshall, i.e. sister to Elder Shubal Stearns). Mercer founded Mercer University (the oldest Baptist-affiliated university in the South) in 1833. Mercer became a prominent voice for the New School Baptists and a strong advocate for missions and ministerial education.

Congregationalist missionaries, Adoniram Judson and Luther Rice. On their way to work with the Englishman William Carey, "father of modern missions," at his India Mission, Judson and Rice were convinced through Bible study that "believer's baptism" was scriptural, and "infant baptism" was unscriptural. Benedict details how their conversion to the Baptists had the effect of challenging Baptist "apathy" concerning missionary activity.

Rice, particularly, was energetic in traveling throughout the southeast to rally Baptists to the cause of evangelizing the lost. He successfully raised significant sums of money for foreign missions, but when he began to redirect those funds to building a school for the training of missionaries, as well as numerous other projects, he became a kind of "lightening rod" for controversy and dissension among those that were previously sympathetic to his ecclesiastical innovations.

It is in Chapter X of this discussion of the 2nd Decade that Benedict elaborates on the tensions between the increasingly polarized groups among the Baptists—groups he labels "Fullerites" and "Gillites":

> FORTY YEARS AGO large bodies of our people were in a state of ferment and agitation, in consequence of some modifications of their old Calvinistic creed, as displayed in the writings of the late Andrew Fuller, of Kettering, England. This famous man maintained that the atonement of Christ was general in its nature, but particular in its application, in opposition to our old divines, who held that Christ died for the elect only. He also made a distinction between the natural and moral inability of men.

Dr. John Gill, of London, was, in his day, one of the most distinguished divines among the English Baptists, and as he was a noted advocate for the old system of a limited atonement, the terms "Gillites" and "Fullerites" were often applied to the parties in this discussion. Those who espoused the views of Mr. Fuller were denominated Arminians by the Gillite men, while they, in their turn, styled their opponents Hyper-Calvinists. Both parties claimed to be orthodox and evangelical, and differed but little on any other points except those which have been named. On Election, the Trinity, etc., they all agreed.

In the age when this discussion arose among the American Baptists, as none of the modern subjects of agitation had been introduced into their churches, the speculative opinions thus briefly described, for a number of years were the occasion of unhappy debates and contentions in many locations.

Our old Baptist divines, especially those of British descent, were generally strong Calvinists as to their doctrinal creed, and but few of them felt at liberty to call upon sinners in plain terms to repent and believe the gospel, on account of their inability to do so without divine assistance. They could preach the gospel before the unconverted, but rousing appeals to their consciences on the subject of their conversion did not constitute a part of their public addresses.

In expatiating on the strong points of their orthodox faith they sometimes ran Calvinism up to seed, and were accused by their opponents of Antinomian tendencies. In that age it was customary for many of our ministers to dwell much on the decrees and purposes of God, to dive deep, in their way, into the plans of Jehovah in eternity, and to bring to light, as they supposed, the hidden treasures of the gospel, which they, in an especial manner, were set to defend. In doing this they discoursed with as much confidence as if they were certain that they were not wise above what is written, but had given a true report of the secrets of the skies.

This extreme of orthodoxy has been followed by laxity and indifference.

The Philadelphia Confession of Faith, published in that city, in 1742, was the standard of most of the oldest Baptist churches in this country, especially in the middle and southern States. This Confession was copied mostly from one published by the Baptists in London, in 1689, and this again agreed in its doctrinal sentiments with the Westminster Confession.

The old Baptists in New England, although, for the most part, they held with their brethren elsewhere the doctrines of Depravity, Election, Divine Sovereignty, Final Perseverance, etc., yet they were not in the habit of enforcing them so strongly as were those in New York, Philadelphia, and further South.

That class of Baptists which arose out of the New-light stir in New England, which, as I have before stated, sent colonies into all the southern States, and in the second generation, over the mountains into the West, were Calvinists of a still milder type. Indeed, their orthodoxy was often called in question by the old school party in Virginia, the Carolinas and Kentucky. These zealous reformers, in their public performances dwelt mostly on the subjects of Christian experience and practical religion, while the strait Calvinists labored much to explain and defend the strong points of their system.

The kind of preaching now much in vogue, at the period and among the people here had in view, would have been considered the quintessence of Arminianism, mere milk and water, instead of the strong meat of the gospel. Then, and with

> our orthodox Baptists, a sermon would have been accounted altogether defective which did not touch upon Election, Total Depravity, Final Perseverance, etc.[24]

Of course, this polarity came to a head in the 1830s, as previously noted. It seems clear that what happened among the American Baptists in the 19th century was a polarization driven by doctrinal differences. The Regulars, as represented by the Philadelphia Association, were theologically-inclined and considered orthodoxy to be the primary concern of the church. The Separates, as represented by the Sandy Creek and Georgia Baptist Association, were more practically-inclined and considered evangelism to be the primary concern of the church. The fissures that developed as the one group accused the other of heresy, and the other accused the one of apathy drove a wedge into the fabric of Baptist culture, effectively splitting the Baptists into two camps.

In the aftermath of the 1832 division, the New School Baptists proceeded to form the Southern Baptist Convention in Augusta, Georgia in 1845. This Convention has since grown into the largest Baptist denomination in the United States of America. The Old School (or Primitive) Baptists, continued the practice of quiet piety and simple worship in independent congregations, comprised of believers in Christ's finished work of redemption and the substantive doctrines of sovereign grace.

During the 20th century, the New School Baptists became almost completely Arminian (or at least semi-Pelagian) in theology, teaching that the Gospel is a free and well-meant offer to unregenerate sinners to be saved, and that the sinner's free-will

---

24 https://www.reformedreader.org/history/benedict/Fifty%20Years%20Among%20the%20Baptists/chapter10.htm

was the determining factor between God's desire to save humanity and the reality of that outcome at an individual level. The preached Gospel is the means by which God's offer of salvation reaches men, according to this view, thereby making the church and the preacher decisive links in the salvation transaction.

Meanwhile, Old School Baptists continued to affirm the finished work of Christ, insisting that the Lord Jesus is not merely a potential or hypothetical Savior that made salvation possible for all, but an actual Savior that secured salvation for all the elect. That legal salvation accomplished at the cross is then vitally and individually applied to every one that was loved by God and chosen in Christ before time began, and the purpose of the Gospel is to nurture the regenerate person in spiritual life, to equip him with the knowledge of God's revealed will and to enlighten the understanding with truth—not to assist the Lord to get sinners saved for heaven.

Happily, the New School ranks have witnessed a recovery (over the past forty years or so) of this emphasis on "sovereign grace," but like the Baptists said of the Reformers, we fear that most "have not reformed far enough." This renewal of emphasis on the covenant of redemption, the doctrines of election and predestination and particular redemption are welcome reforms indeed. Still, however, the preoccupation with the Fullerite notion that the Gospel is a well-meant offer of salvation and either the means by which regeneration occurs, or a virtually simultaneous event with regeneration, does not lend itself to the prospect of walking together in gospel unity again. That remaining tension, notwithstanding, I can applaud and rejoice whenever Christ is truly preached by those in other traditions and communions.

Summary

This small volume is an attempt to sketch some of the key developments in Christian history for the benefit of the average believer. Professional scholars and accomplished historians may take issue with an omission here and there, or an editorial interpretation I have made concerning a particular event, but I have labored to be accurate in the record and sequence of events cited and to document my source information as much as possible.

My primary objective in this work is to clearly emphasize that just as the Lord Jesus promised in Matthew 16:18 that "*the gates of hell* [would] *not prevail against*" his church, that promise has not failed. A witness to the truth of God has continued in the earth since the days of Christ and his apostles.

The second point I wish the reader to glean from these pages is that the longevity of the New Testament Church is due to nothing short of the providence of God. With all of its flaws, miscues, idiosyncrasies, eccentricities, deviations, divisions and errors through the centuries, nothing but the Supernatural power of God the Holy Spirit should be credited with the perpetuity of his church throughout the ages.

Finally, I pray the reader will not fault me for stating my honest, personal conviction that, though they are obscure and frequently dismissed as irrelevant in the larger conversation of modern Christendom, the Primitive Baptists, generally speaking, in distinction to other Christian groups, even among the Baptists, possess the identifying marks of the apostolic New Testament Church, both in doctrine and in practice. I deem it to be the highest privilege of my life to be numbered among them.

www.ingramcontent.com/pod-product-compliance
Lightning Source LLC
LaVergne TN
LVHW091001080826
845145LV00003B/1088

* 9 7 8 1 9 2 9 6 3 5 3 8 2 *